WARNER BROS

James Cagney, 1938—part dancer, part boxer; from wisecrack to break your face—the essential Warners actor and the sweetest guy on the lot

Warner Bros

The Making of an
American Movie Studio

DAVID THOMSON

Yale

UNIVERSITY
PRESS

New Haven and London

Yale University Press books may be purchased in quantity for educational,
business, or promotional use. For information, please e-mail sales.press@yale.edu
(U.S. office) or sales@yaleup.co.uk (U.K. office).

Set in Janson Oldstyle type by Integrated Publishing Solutions.
Printed in the United States of America.

Library of Congress Control Number: 2016956162
ISBN 978-0-300-19760-0 (hardcover : alk. paper)

A catalogue record for this book is available from the British Library.

This paper meets the requirements of ANSI/NISO Z39.48-1992
(Permanence of Paper).

10 9 8 7 6 5 4 3 2

For Sam Hamm, who gave Warner Bros a boost
in its declining years
For Michael Barker, who did the same for me
For Chuck Jones—"What's up, Doc?"—who treated us all

CONTENTS

CONTENTS

1

An Introduction: Families and Stories

FAMILIES ARE ALIKE, whatever they say. They start to talk, to gossip or complain, and soon that turns into stories; we have to do that much, or sit there in silence. The narratives that spring up want to be unique and personal, but they are leaves from one tree. There are only a few stories if we regard them as shapes made out of possibility, rites of fear and desire. This condition lasted mankind from the cave to the cabin, but then story itself took flight. A few families broke into the business of enacting those stories for *strangers*—audiences who might be far away, but the new technology reached them. The stories existed as coiled celluloid, waiting to be freed by light. This one family, the Warners, helped create that business and left us believing that their stories were our fables and dreams, and not just their money and their made-up name.

This book is called *Warner Bros*, but if anyone asks, you're going to say you're reading "Warner Brothers." You don't quite know how to say "Warner Bros." That logo seems awkward or compacted in the mouth. This is not a trivial distinction between sound and print, family and business identity. They didn't call themselves Paramount or Universal or Columbia, names from out of the clouds. No, they said theirs was a family show, just the brothers, one for all and all for one.

There really were four Warner brothers, and if Albert was a sleeping or sleepy partner, Harry, Sam, and Jack are genuine characters. Sam takes an early hit for the team, and that makes him a beloved hero, but Harry and Jack carry the load of lifelong rivalry, like Karamazov brothers, vectors to build a story arc on. They fall into unthinking opposition. Why do we have siblings? they wonder—So there's someone close to us who is *not* us?

Jack wins this fraternal struggle—you'll guess that early on, so no suspense is spoiled. But so many of his victories feel like defeats, too, because of his suspect character. He's known as a rascal now, while Harry seems upright and duty-bound. Harry could read and write in Hebrew, while Jack struggled with English. But it's too late to take sides: Harry may have been more honest, but he was dull, too; and if Jack was shifty, that was why you shouldn't take your eyes off him. The two of them seem always at odds, which leaves victorious Jack as maybe the biggest scumbag ever to get into a Jewish Lives series. I realize "scumbag" is startling: it doesn't sound judicious; and it may be disconcerting to have a Jewish Life that isn't admirable, or couched in integrity. Einstein, Freud, Proust, Primo Levi, Kafka, Emma Goldman . . . Jack Warner? But this subject is more important than respectability.

I said "scumbag" for a couple of reasons—Jack *is* something other than a nobleman; but "scumbag" is a familiar term in the movie business, where it carries more affection than if it were being bandied about in insurance or undertaking. Hollywood, you see, is fond of its rascals, rather in the way we relish its villains or tough guys on screen when they are people we would be scared to meet. And that hints at the complicated influence the Warner brothers had, and are still having, on us. Here's a question to illustrate that: which means the most to the most people, or to you: the Special Theory of Relativity, Freud's *The Interpretation of Dreams*, or Jimmy Cagney pushing a grapefruit in Mae Clarke's face?

I cannot tell you Jack was a hero, or that many who knew him made that claim on his behalf. But being less than Einstein, Proust, or even Barbra Streisand didn't stop Jack and Warner Bros from having an impact on our culture and dreams, on us, that is alarming because it's enormous. Warner Bros was one of the enterprises that helped us see there might be an American dream out there, a mix of patriotism and publicity, and it was open to Poles, Hispanics, the British and Chinese, whomever, as much as to the few Americans who had been here from the start. Even women might get it. That sense of a dream and immigrants—enormous, impersonal, climatic forces—is not easily worked out because we are still so attached to the hope that fine and talented people shape our history. Or very bad people? Don't rule this out as simple heresy, but America might have been happier without the pursuit of happiness.

Once upon a time, nearly everyone lived in his or her small, fixed place. You could not get away, so you hardly felt the need—you were contained in the power of heaven and hell, or some such script. Then transport shook us up. It began as railways, steamships, and automobiles, as well as money. It has gone on by way of the telephone and radio to our modern capacity or fantasy for being anywhere. But this transition has been a convulsion; it has driven people crazy and it means we lost godliness, as well as home.

This was happening all over the world, but in the United States the throb of fiction or future becoming was a frenzy as, in the last decades of the nineteenth century, millions of strangers came to the country and complicated its old New England ideals. That immigrant anxiety, over feeling freed yet lost, has never gone away, but in America a mass medium was set up, for fun but as a version of moral guidance and comfort: the stories told people how to live, or what to believe in—stay a family, they sometimes urged. But the technology was dynamic and disruptive, too: it catered to loneliness, instability, and escape and said such things were as natural as home and allegiance. The messages strove to be wholesome, and conservative, but families like the Warners had escaped, so they loved the danger-ous energy that needed. The contradictions were riotous—for example, crime does not pay, they said, but get ready to enjoy these hoodlums of ours! And in that process these men repre-sented all immigrants. They were storytellers who dramatized the vitality of instability and transformation. They were the actors who played the role of strangers in the land. And, don't forget, some "true" Americans still look upon immigrants with suspicion and fear.

Another point of the title, *Warner Bros*, is to say that this genius is collective as well as individual, and that is a challeng-ing theory in both film history and the progress of artistic ap-preciation. You can take a film like *Casablanca* and ask, who made it? If *Casablanca* ends up being taught at Cornell or a ju-nior college for credit and tenure, then it helps to pin it on an author. But maybe so many people made the picture that no one deserves the credit—perhaps *we* did it.

Criticism and tenure are alike in needing heroes. There are important (and self-important) individuals in this book—not just Jack Warner but Darryl Zanuck, James Cagney, Bette Davis, Humphrey Bogart, Howard Hawks . . . Bugs Bunny—and there will be times when their talent and their choices stand out from the body of the institution. But this is also a book in which general weather systems—like sound, a factory system for storytelling, business, rivalry, the sounds of song and gun-fire, and the shuffling off of responsibility—take priority.

The thing called "audience" may be the most profound and mysterious of those forces. "Audience" is a lovely and be-guiling idea, and sometimes it is enough to scatter those darker versions of the same principle—the public, the crowd, the mass, the others. One of the essential areas of intrigue in going to the movies, of sitting in the dark with strangers, was feeling the show was just for you—yet guessing you didn't matter. Be-cause the bright life on the screen didn't know or care if you existed. So long as you paid your nickel, or your $16.

In coming to this task, it feels proper to raise a question, or an eyebrow, at the mention of Harry, Abe, Sam—and Jack? Even the *shvontz*—the prick? Are we sure of where we're going with these Warner boys?

What do we expect of a Jewish Life? Surely the publishing test isn't based on the mere existence of anyone who happened to be Jewish? I doubt the editors of this series would proceed to print a full account of what might be plain or empty lives—say, Isaac of Prague (1171–1262), or Hirsch Wonsal (1781–1858), the one a tailor, the other a shoemaker, lacking not just English, but American, too, dots in that unstable eastern part of Europe, buffeted or chased by fierce ethnic disputes in which they had no say and so little record that a "Life" is beyond telling.

Those two names—Isaac and Hirsch are both invented—could be signifiers for lives that left hardly a trace of evidence and which we may assume to have been commonplace (dull?), subject to passing happiness and terror, but resigned to history having no reason to remember or identify their small "hill of beans." These were not prophets, scholars, creative artists, or leaders—if they had genius, it went unnoticed (and that can happen—must everything hang on the test of success or fame?). It is the pattern of history and the tradition of our evolutionary culture that many lives are not much attended to—except by the Lord, or Yahweh. Unless those overseers are just figures in storytelling.

But Warner Bros movies were for all of us. Yiddish theatre might be for the Jews, but the movies were for everyone. You didn't have to be Orthodox or saved to buy your ticket. And these brothers longed to transcend Jewishness, and the traditions that they thought made them vulnerable in America.

There was a movie made in 1947, *Gentleman's Agreement*.[1] It was not from Warners, and it is not well remembered now. Nevertheless, it won the Best Picture Oscar for 1947, and was once reckoned to be on a cutting edge because it exposed anti-semitism. It is a story in which a sincere journalist (played by Gregory Peck) pretends to be Jewish to report on that cultural hostility. The film has dated (a smaller film, same year, similar theme, *Crossfire*, is superior). But in 1947 someone organized a gathering of Hollywood elders to impress upon Darryl Zanuck (the film's producer) that it was ill-advised and unduly provocative to stir up this issue. The instigator of that meeting was Jack Warner, who preferred to make Jewishness go away as a brand image.

Zanuck was not Jewish, and he is essential to the Warners story. He was of Swiss, Protestant descent (he said), born in Wahoo, Nebraska. His father was a hotel clerk who claimed the principles of Episcopalianism, while being a drunk and a gambler who neglected his son. A stepfather came along later, an accountant and another drunk who carried a Bible for quoting from. But Darryl discarded these parents to spend his working life with people who were Jewish, and it was often said that he topped them all in behaving *as if Jewish*, or the way a movie mogul was expected to behave.

In 1967, when Zanuck was once more in charge of Twentieth Century–Fox, John Gregory Dunne went to interview him in his New York office. He found what he wanted—a tough character, a onetime scenarist, talking splashy dialogue:

"I'm so goddamn sick of being written about. What the hell am I going to say about myself that I haven't said before?" groaned Zanuck.[2] It's a tyrant's lament that would fit most of our demon moguls, from Louis B. Mayer to . . . Donald Trump.

As studio president in New York, Zanuck was in daily contact with his son Richard, the man he had appointed head of production in Los Angeles, and the kid Darryl had always beaten at checkers, croquet, or any other game anyone could think of: "I was put under terrific criticism when I sent Dick out to head up the studio. What could I do? He was the only one I could trust. . . . Well, when I took over, I cleaned house. I knew things were bad, but not that bad. I paid off millions of dollars in contracts and threw out every goddamn script we had in preparation. They were all lousy. And then I sent Dick out there. I let him alone."[3]

Trust the rhythm of the paranoia and its assertion more than what is claimed; listen to the act. For all his house-cleaning, Darryl Zanuck had kept the studio attached to *Doctor Dolittle*, *Star!*, and *Tora! Tora! Tora!*, and when those films flopped, three in a row, he had to fire someone—so he fired Dick. Beware of family.

For a man of five feet six, Zanuck had always cast a big shadow. He revered his wife and his kids, but got into the early habit of sex with young actresses. He believed in himself, his instincts, his will, and his luck. His mouth clenched a cigar while firing off indefatigable show business lines full of panache. These were wisecrack howlers like the infamous remarks of Sam Goldwyn. Zanuck was at a preview once, at Warners, in the early thirties, with the film's director, Michael Curtiz. Zanuck was in charge of production at Warners then. He felt there was something wrong with this picture they were watching. He tried to spell out what it was, and the anxious Curtiz leaped in with "Wonderful! Darryl! Yes! Yes!" Whereupon Zanuck glared at his unquenchable yes man, and said, "For Christ's sake, don't say yes until I finish talking!"[4]

Was that Jewish—or simply the kind of sizzling line that a boss might utter in a Hollywood picture (especially one directed by Michael Curtiz)? It's a laugh line; it's an assertion of authority, and it's memorable—it illustrates a way of talking in life that owes a lot to sound pictures. The line rides along with "You ain't heard nothin' yet!" from *The Jazz Singer* (for which Zanuck won an honorary Oscar as its controlling mastermind).

Everyone agreed with Darryl Zanuck that he was not Jewish—and people didn't expect to win arguments with him. But how many people did you ever hear of who were called "Zanuck," and might have come from Switzerland? Is Zanuck a Swiss name, or is it just the most punchy, catchy handle in the picture business? Darryl was blue-eyed and fair-haired; he was from out of Nebraska. According to Orson Welles, he was also "by all odds the best and brightest of the big studio bosses."[5]

In passing, recollect that Orson Welles sometimes wondered whether both his parents were the advertised article—as in straight Americans; as an orphan, he was significantly raised by a Jewish guardian; he did wonder whether his mother had known a dashing Jewish actor; and he was inclined to rave about the glories of Yiddish literature and theatre—"It was the only international theatre in history. Movies are the second."[6]

This alchemy is crucial in the transactions by which strangers become Americans when the rest of the world regards the United States as a reckless, slightly disturbed, but beckoning mélange of so many races and nationalities that have not really had time or boredom to be American yet. The cultural importance of the movies was in presenting a persuasive model for style and authenticity, and no group had more to do with that than the Jews who established the picture business. Maybe living creatures as diverse as Cary Grant and Rin Tin Tin found themselves as American role models. Grant, who had grown up as Archie Leach in Bristol, England, with a father named Elias, believed he might be "partly" Jewish. The great Rinty (America's favorite canine) was actually a French German shepherd puppy, found by an American soldier in the village of Flirey in Lorraine in September 1918. That dog soon became a hero in Warner Brothers films, some of them written by Darryl Zanuck. For much of his life, Charlie Chaplin flirted with the thought that he could have been Jewish.[7] The American movie is a lever in the reinvention of the self—and its eternal discontent with fixed reality.

This spreading confusion of identities is a measure of collapsing times. We'll see, because the process continues. But in the Warner Brothers we face an attempt—organic but crazy, yearning yet hardly planned—by early-twentieth-century Jews to be American. That's how Zanuck—ten years his junior—had such an influence on Jack Warner. And whereas Harry, Albert, and Sam were escaped from eastern Europe, their kid brother, Jack, was show business or North American.

That's not to attack Jack, or to excuse him, but it's surely relevant that these Warner brothers lived at a moment when the world was suddenly aroused by the question of what it meant to be Jewish. In so many respects, the substance of spiritual belief was disappearing in the West. But at the same time a new urge to tell stories arose—stories that were parables on community and individualism, success and responsibility. The thing Orson Welles noted—the way in which Yiddish storytelling produced and was then supplanted by the movies—meant that in a culture abandoning religion, myths were made fresh and accessible to the ragbag of Americans. Those stories taught immigrants English—and a thought of being American.

John Ford's *The Searchers* (1956) is clearly a Western, with American archetypes who happen to be caught up in racial confusion with Native American characters. Still, the brothers in the film are named Aaron and Ethan, American names that do not always hear how Jewish they are (and these brothers loved the same woman, Martha—it is her daughter who is kidnapped, thus prompting the search).[8]

For generations, children were named after lives from the Bible, as if that gave a kid roots, moral identity, and a basis for behaving. Modern American lives do not know the Bible in the same way—I don't think the average viewer of *The Searchers* in 2017 hears the biblical resonance. But such echoes linger because some model for family existence remains from biblical structures in which brothers might be so bound together in contest that sometimes one may have to murder the other.

Harold Pinter's *The Homecoming* (1965)—to pick another Jewish artist—is a piece of sinister, allegorical stagecraft, about a family's struggle for power. It plays as an abstract noir fable of north London life, in which sibling rivalry never sleeps. A prized son, Teddy (learned but childlike), returns (from America), with his prized wife (Ruth), only to realize that his supposedly lesser family members are still wolves waiting for him to falter. They are his father Max; an uncle, Sam; and Teddy's two brothers, Lenny and Joey. Ruth becomes the all-purpose anima for the family. The father and her brothers-in-law first try to co-opt her as their whore, but that shows her the power she could have in a home where the men lack women. She will stay in London like a queen, a madam, and a mother, while the defeated Teddy goes back to America.

The Searchers and *The Homecoming* may not seem to come from the same cultural source. But their secret kinship and their obsession with family rivalry speak to the influence of Jewish storytelling—and Pinter loved movies. So Teddy comes home to be eclipsed. But Ethan (even as personified by John Wayne) goes on an immense quest in which we fear he may kill his defiled niece if he ever finds her—a relationship all the more fraught if he might be her father (which surely he wanted to be). When Ethan accepts Debbie and brings her "home," he turns away at the threshold and walks back into the desert, without existence. He has erased himself. It was a Warner Brothers movie.

In 1988, Neal Gabler published a notable book, *An Empire of Their Own: How the Jews Invented Hollywood*, which described how a group of Jews had made what we call the American movie business. This reading was valid and useful, though it failed to explore how fully the American public had acclaimed and digested Hollywood, and whether or not the moguls understood that or were really in charge of the process. Neither the business nor the imaginative enterprise was simply "an empire of their own."

Instead, it was an uneasy kingdom in which Jewish moguls were often in fear of exposure and attack. And they did not have to be Jewish. The character of Hollywood and of Warners owed so much to Darryl Zanuck, and the list of vital non-Jews begins with D. W. Griffith, Cecil B. DeMille, Mary Pickford and Lillian Gish, Walt Disney, John Ford, Alfred Hitchcock— and even Chaplin, or Jock Whitney. Jock (or John Hay) Whitney was maybe the most famous WASP in America in 1939, and one of the richest. But David Selznick could not have made *Gone With the Wind* without Jock. That worked because a part of Whitney wanted to shed his worthy heritage, wanted to adventure, meet movie stars (actresses especially), and play with being an outsider.

Yes, there were many Jews in Hollywood (but the business was never all Jews) and they were powerful for a time, enough to feel a new version of being "chosen." The lasting power rested in what the uncontrolled and un-understood technology was doing to American hope. Along the way to power and their sometimes lurid splendor, these moguls compromised many of the hallowed meanings of Jewish life beginning around, say, 1900. That's how Harry Warner would be ashamed of his young brother Jack. The "empire" was less a dynasty than an escape struggling to regain or reinvent home. These immigrants were American now, but "home" was up for redesign. The country is still torn over the battle to decide whose story it will be.

2

The Greatest Moment?

IT'S NO SECRET: *Casablanca* is the most celebrated movie made by Warners, and one of the most cherished ever created in Hollywood. Not that the ordinary fans necessarily identified a picture with its studio. The ownership credit on a movie is usu ally one of the least noticed bits of information. As an audience, we like to think a picture belongs to us.

In 1943, that spirit rejoiced, along with the gamblers who ran Warners, that Allied forces had occupied the real Casablanca (in Morocco) just weeks before the movie opened. That emphatic yet romantic title seemed vindicated by the news. Wouldn't we always have "Casablanca"? There were maps of North Africa on newspaper front pages to settle widespread ignorance as to where the city was. In addition, as one screenwriter put it, in January 1942, the film vouched for "the idea that when people lose faith in their ideals, they are beaten before they begin to fight."[1] This was a respectable message, lofty but vague, but one that made us feel good about ourselves in 1943, when feeling good came more easily than it does now.

Here was a movie about success and togetherness, those essential Hollywood convictions. That appealed to the brothers named Warner, as it did to the immigrant generation that had founded the picture business and who assumed that their own social transformation was a principle that could be sold to millions (if not exactly shared with them).

When *Casablanca* won its Best Picture Oscar, the man who felt he deserved to collect the statuette was the film's producer and chief manager, Hal B. (for Brent) Wallis. If anyone had run the whole show of that picture, and kept its untidiness under control, it was Wallis. Even if it had not always been under control, Wallis was the leader who smothered the doubts.[2]

He had been born in Chicago in 1898, the son of Ashkenazi Jews from Suwalki in Poland, who had named him Aaron Blum Wolowicz, before they changed the family name to Wallis. Hal had joined Warners in 1923, doing publicity in a lowly position, and had risen gradually to be head of production. That was how the business could work. By 1939, he had won the Irving G. Thalberg Award for production excellence, because he was— or seemed to be—in charge of one of the most impressive lists of movies ever created in Hollywood. In the 1930s and early forties, Warners had had nineteen films nominated for Best Picture—and they had actually won that Oscar once, for *The Life of Emile Zola*, which was as much a gloss on the history of ideas as *Casablanca* was a slick version of war studies.

But that Oscars night in 1943, Wallis was beaten to the Academy stage by his own boss, Jack Warner, a man famous for speed, opportunism, ego, and the rueful jokes told by those who worked under him and endured his constant appetite for attention and audience response. As Hal was going towards the stage, Jack leaped forward to take the statuette himself. "Jack L. Warner" was meant to sound like a reliable American name (he adopted it in his brief vaudeville career, when middle initials had a rhythmic kick like the flourish on a snare drum). But he was born Jacob to Jews from Congress Poland (the Russian end of that unhappy country), his father either Wonsal or Wonskolasor at his own birth. Jacob had been born in London, Ontario, in 1892, as his family moved around seeking a home in the New World.

Casablanca had been directed by Michael Curtiz, born in Budapest in 1886 as Mano Kaminer, who then became Mihaly Kertesz as he made his way in the European film business. Under any name he was Jewish.[3] He arrived in America in 1926, settled on an American name, and, thanks to a shared passion for polo, formed a friendship with Hal Wallis. It's a pretty prospect to think of these two ex-Europeans, tanned and pristine, on polo ponies. Curtiz was something of a joke at Warners, infamous for his aloof manner, his arrogance, his skill at moving the camera, and his broken English. As he often admitted (and as his bosses complained), he was more concerned with cinematic style than with character, plot, or dialogue—yet *Casablanca* is not simply a fast, elegant romantic thriller made for a moment in history; it is full of characters and lines we remember. Along the way, Curtiz directed a bunch of admirable American movies, nearly all at Warners—*20,000 Years in Sing Sing* (Spencer Tracy and Bette Davis), *Mystery of the Wax Museum* (a horror film), *Captain Blood* and *The Adventures of Robin Hood* (both with Errol Flynn), *Angels with Dirty Faces* (Cagney and Bogart), *The Private Lives of Elizabeth and Essex* (Davis and Flynn), *Casablanca*, *Yankee Doodle Dandy* (where Cagney won his Oscar playing impresario George M. Cohan), *Mildred Pierce* (the noir romance in which Joan Crawford got her Oscar), *Life with Father* (a family movie and a great hit, starring William Powell).

Even this selected list of pictures suggests that Curtiz's greatest characteristic was versatility, or the ability to do whatever the studio required with the same brisk flourish and an expertise in never being boring. Yet no one knew what a Curtiz picture was, and in the culture of critics who wish to celebrate the movie director, and call him an auteur, Curtiz is a problem. His record is prodigious, but impersonal, so it reflects strangely on directorial signature.

Curtiz directed most of *Casablanca*—except for bits here and there, like the montage sequence that establishes the city as a place and mood, which was actually assembled by Don Siegel because he had the speed, the zip, and the skill to do all the studio montages.[4] Warners favored those snappy montages as much as any studio (though you can see the same spirit at work in the obituary sequence in *Citizen Kane*), because they established a story in a few seconds and let the public feel that the news and history were under control.

But the writing of a movie was another matter, even if screenwriting at Warners was intended to convey a similar sense of authority in which doubt had been chased away. A lot of the time on *Casablanca* the studio and its workers hardly knew where the picture was going, but they knew that uncertainty must never show. Four men played significant parts in the writing, and maybe forty were asked to take a shot at certain scenes. In the crises of filmmaking, emergency writers may be called in to do scenes or doctor those already written. An individual writer may have no idea of the confusion or treachery in which he is working—it helps not to know. So Julius Epstein, who cowrote with his twin brother, Philip, asserted that Casey Robinson had never written a draft, and while Howard Koch did about thirty pages, Epstein said they were bad and never used. Yet Robinson claimed that he had recommended the play *Everybody Comes to Rick's* (even though his account of the play is inaccurate). He also said he had clarified, or "punched up," the love story. And he was the creator of the ending (put off for so long), while admitting that Hal Wallis himself wrote that last line, as Rick and Renault stroll off into the fog, "Louis, I think this is the beginning of a beautiful friendship."[5]

It's impossible to get the history straight, and that may be because the rivalrous authors themselves never knew exactly what had happened—and wouldn't have remembered it if they had. Wallis employed a lot of writers, to get talent, and to keep it insecure. And here we are into the willful chaos of Warner Brothers—and all the other movie studios. Someone like Hal Wallis had to drag the broken pieces together and turn them into what Julius Epstein called "Slick shit."[6]

Julius offered that verdict in an interview decades later on a picture for which he and his brother had shared the adapted screenplay Oscar with Howard Koch. No, he said, "Slick shit" didn't mean he hated or despised *Casablanca*. But he had no illusions. There wasn't a jot of reality in the whole picture, if reality was what had actually transpired in North Africa during the war. The movie was a fantasy cobbled together that happened to work. What else was a sane writer with self-respect to say about the process? Epstein was a sardonic wit, very good at a job he seldom thought respectable. So he talked about it as a hooker might discuss her johns—amused, forgetful, fatalistic, and with a touch of superior disdain. That jaunty toughness is very Warner Brothers, and it's a voice we can follow over the years. Screenwriters trained themselves not to take their own pages or hopes too seriously because they could be trashed, abandoned, or lost. "Slick shit" was a wry defensive attitude, and it's not so far from the way Rick oversees the customers and the losers at his café.

I'm sure Casey Robinson had a useful hand in *Casablanca*, but he never got a credit—and who knows the arrangements that went into that denial? So the script was attributed to the Epstein brothers and Howard Koch. If only the film had failed, there might have been just a single credit. Writers dodge flops and make a crowded elevator if the picture is going up in the world.

But when interviewed by Patrick McGilligan, Julius Epstein was asked where his wry humor—heard especially in the cheerful cynicism of Captain Renault (Claude Rains)—had come from. He replied, with a laugh:

"From being Jewish."

McGilligan asked him to elaborate and Epstein replied, "Who knows? I have no explanation for it." He refers to two books by Steve Allen, *Funny People* and *More Funny People*, and he says, "His only explanation is that it must come in the genes, because the only way the Jews could last all the years is by laughing at it. . . . You know what Lenny Bruce said? Everybody on the two coasts, by which he meant New York and Los Angeles, is Jewish. Everyone in between is gentile. In other words, he meant if you're in show business or if you *think* alike you're Jewish."[7]

No one forgets who acted in *Casablanca*. Those dead faces are still alive—was that always the deepest reason why people wanted to be in movies? There are folklore tales about all the actors considered for every part, but that was standard procedure on most projects in the studio system. If you had players under long-term contract, then you had to use them or play with the prospects of using them. Casting was a version of the other game in which a mogul might survey the pretty young women under contract before deciding which one to call to his office at 4 p.m. So yes, there was a story in January 1942, just weeks after Warners had bought the rights to the play, that Ronald Reagan and Ann Sheridan would star in *Casablanca*. But in the first reader's report on the play, in mid-December 1941, days after Pearl Harbor, there had been this recommendation: "A boxoffice natural—for Bogart, or Cagney, or Raft in out-of-the-usual roles, and perhaps Mary Astor."[8]

Casting a movie requires exhilarated indecision, always on the brink of panic—after all, it's Friday and by Monday morning *someone* has to be there as Rick or Ilsa. Once that's accomplished, the movie can appear as sublime providence. Who else could it have been? Bogart and Ingrid Bergman *are* the two people now. Yet it might have been George Raft and Michele Morgan, for one moment at least. Then everyone would know who Michele Morgan was—she died in December 2016. Hal Wallis always had Bogart in mind, but Ilsa was up in the air. She could have been French, English, or American. Come to that, Wallis had a passing urge to turn Sam, the piano player, into a woman, and he thought of Lena Horne in the part.[9] To learn that is to waver over fate, and to feel indignant on behalf of Dooley Wilson—but Lena Horne had her grievances with Hollywood, too. (And that song, "As Time Goes By," means something a little different if you have any hint that Rick might have been "seeing" a young singer who looked and sounded like Horne. Rick joins the noble cause in *Casablanca*, but could he have had sex with a woman of color? Just how liberal was Warner Brothers in 1943?)

I share these stories (and the speculation that wraps them) just to stress a mystery in all movies: how a floating role can become iconic in half a day's shooting. So actors had every reason to feel insecure: Bogart had as healthy and sarcastic a dislike of Jack Warner as anyone on the lot. But a big element in the charm of *Casablanca* is that underlying air of comradeship, and of an international cast coming together at a moment when everyone was appreciating how the war was turning strangers into allies. If you run through the cast of aliens for this very American film, you realize that Bogart and Dooley Wilson were the only Americans with sizable roles.

Ingrid Bergman was Swedish; Claude Rains and Sydney Greenstreet were English; Paul Henreid was Austrian, and nearly an aristocrat. It's another part of the airy kindness in

Casablanca that Henreid's Victor Laszlo is said to have been in a concentration camp for a year before the picture opens. To be sure, he has an elegant scar on his brow as "proof" of that experience. But Henreid is handsome, groomed, dentally secure, and possessor of an unshakable confidence, as befits an actor on the rise in a good role in what felt like a hit. Laszlo says he was tortured in the camp when he looks like an actor on the edge of becoming a romantic lead. That's part of a sweetness in the film that belies every allegation that its world faced horrific crisis.

Better proof of that is Laszlo's enemy, Major Strasser, as embodied by the German actor Conrad Veidt. I admit a secret fondness for Strasser, but I think you do, too. Yes, he's a bad man, the Nazi incarnate, imperious but riding for a fall, and probably far worse than the movie has time to show. On the other hand, on our screen's surface, he is polite, urbane, witty even, and well-spoken. And as handsome as Conrad Veidt. We are meant to be afraid of him, but that never quite works for me because this whole gathering of actors becomes a club, inspired by the slick shit they are putting together. They are like the "usual suspects" referred to in Renault's famous line about police procedure. You can argue that in 1942 not too many people had an adequate idea of what a Nazi officer might be like. But the bond in the cast is also a Hollywood attitude: that this is a war movie a child or a childish person could see without damage or undue fear.

It happens that, despite an appearance that could easily seem sinister, Veidt was a good or decent man, liked by anyone he worked with. Born in Berlin in 1893, he had been a leading actor in German cinema: he is the somnambulist in *The Cabinet of Dr. Caligari* and the man whose face has been disfigured into an endless smile in *The Man Who Laughs*. He quit Germany when the Nazis came to power, because his third wife was Jewish. He had gone to England and starred in *The Spy in Black* and *The Thief of Bagdad*. So now, in the orthodoxy of profiling, this tall, handsome man was cast as the Nazi leader. Years earlier, a similar thing had happened to Erich von Stroheim. As a very humble Austrian, without a von to his name, Stroheim had arrived in Hollywood to be cast as Hun baddies, and to advise on the correct details of Prussian uniforms.

Because he had to be on loan from MGM, Veidt earned $5,000 a week, nearly twice Bogart's salary. Such ironies ran through the supporting cast. Peter Lorre, born Laszlo Lowenstein in Hungary, has the modest role of Ugarte. He had become a star playing the murderer in Fritz Lang's *M*, so the movie business took it for granted that he must always be a villain or a madman. In America, Lorre had played the Japanese detective Mr. Moto in eight B pictures in the space of three years—an escape, but a prison, too. He had been Joel Cairo (with Bogart, Greenstreet, and Mary Astor) in *The Maltese Falcon*. He was friendly with Bogart, but that meant he had to realize that he would never be a star and was usually cast as a disturbed person with wicked or craven designs.

There is a croupier at Rick's Café Américain. It's a small role, filled by Marcel Dalio, who had served Jean Renoir as one of the escaping prisoners in *La Grande Illusion* and then played the marquis in *La Règle du Jeu*. That is one of the great performances in French cinema, a superb creation of uneasy nobility, the master of the house but a kid with his elaborate toys, a guilty husband and avid womanizer. Marcel Dalio was an exceptional actor. But he was Jewish (born Israel Moshe Blauschild), and in 1940 he left France for America. He was welcomed by studios who may not have seen his Renoir films and could not see how he was fit to play lead roles. And so here he is a croupier who can magic his roulette wheel and turn up 22 when Rick gives him the nod. That nod is an insiders' sentimental expression of understanding and loyalty between the two men, as beautiful but unspoken a friendship as that between Rick and Sam. In life, after Dalio had left France, the Germans posted close-up posters of him on Parisian streets saying, "This is what a Jew looks like."

The good turn that Dalio's croupier manages in the film is so that a pretty young woman can purchase liberty for herself and her husband, instead of having to sell herself for a night or two to Captain Renault. That actress was Joy Page (born Paige), and it seems that she got the sentimental part on her own. But her stepfather was Jack Warner, who wanted to do nothing to encourage or mislead her, so he made sure she was paid less than any other speaking-part actor in the film. And that Joy Page never made another film for Warners. You may think that's because she was the child of Jack's second wife from an earlier marriage. Not at all; Jack also did whatever he could to discourage his own son, Jack Jr., the kid who shouldn't really have had that name if he was meant to be a regular Jewish son.

Elsewhere in *Casablanca*, you will find S. Z. Sakall, Jewish and born in Hungary. Sakall had worked in German cinema until 1933, when he chose to return to Hungary. By 1940, he thought it wise to move on to America. Wallis picked him to play the headwaiter at Rick's, and he did a fine job. It led to another fifteen years' work as a supporting player in Hollywood. He was known as "Cuddles." But most of his immediate family, including three sisters, had died in concentration camps.

Do you remember the singer, Yvonne, who has had an affair with Rick? She was played by Madeleine Lebeau, who had fled from France in 1940 with Marcel Dalio. They had married in 1939. They managed to get to Lisbon and with forged papers (or letters of transit), they sailed to Chile and made their way north to Hollywood and *Casablanca*. It sounds like a romantic story—it sounds like *Casablanca* itself, where Yvonne leads the singing of La Marseillaise with shiny tears in her eyes—but the couple divorced before the film opened. Lebeau died only in May 2016, the last survivor from the picture.

Then there's the barman at the café. His role had been cast.

Leo Mostovoy was playing the part, until he struck observers as too earnest or lacking in a natural comedic sense. Curtiz and Wallis sought a strain of sardonic humor whenever possible. So Mostovoy was replaced with Leonid Kinskey, born in St. Petersburg in 1903 and compelled to leave his country because he was no supporter of the Revolution. He found small parts as an actor, but he got the barman role because he was one of the entourage Bogart liked to drink with.

So there was a ganglike air on the film, and Warner Brothers in the 1930s had made some of the best gang films ever done. No one involved on the picture could miss the unusual league of nations and refugees that had been enlisted. And whatever the uncertainty over the script, everyone could guess that Max Steiner (a Viennese Jew) would come in at the end with a score so adept at romance, suspense, and sheer swagger that the film would soar. Steiner was at Warners for thirty years, and he wrote music for 140 films. It was his stuff that played over the opening WB logo. He is vital to the atmosphere of the studio, whether we call the result slick shit or inspiring entertainment.

There was no mistaking *Casablanca* as a Warners production, but to what extent was it a Jewish film? That's a question to bear in mind while understanding that Warners were anxious not to seem like a Jewish business. They wanted to be American, and hoped that role existed. So it was a film that addressed the justice and necessity of the war, and was pledged to the idea of America as a proper part of the Allied effort. But the Jewish experience of the war was not emphasized. There is a flashback to Rick and Ilsa in Paris that is fair enough, though not the best scene in the picture and not quite necessary. But there is no glimpse of Laszlo in a concentration camp. It's more to the point, and closer to the theme of this book, that the film was liberal in its sentiments, brilliant and appealing in its screen decisiveness, wry, fond of sentiment yet hardboiled, as if to say we're Americans, we can take it and dish it out, we're the best, tough and soft at the same time. So much of that crazed package of attractive attitudes came from the movies and passed into the nervous system of the country.

I should add that I am not Jewish (or quite American). Some things ameliorate that and may serve as credentials (or letters of transit). When I was four, in London, my grannie showed me newspaper pictures of the relief of concentration camps, and tried to explain those images. I was filled with awe and terror, and I know that the Holocaust (which I could not grasp then) has been the most important cultural event in my life. It still is; it ensures that a child's horror persists.

Some of us know what Sylvia Plath meant in her poem "Daddy," when she said, "I think I may well be a Jew."[10] But here's a dilemma: Sylvia Plath was a rage for a while in the years after she died. That was fifty-four years ago. It won't be long before the last survivors of the concentration camps are gone, too. Then history takes its rest: the outrages of the Hundred Years' War are merely notional now. What century was that? We have to accept that the hard facts of 1939–45 will go into soft focus. I know, that's regrettable, or deplorable. Trickier by far is the way *Casablanca* endures and becomes a passive, fraudulent version of what happened in the war. Yet the loyalists of movies still tell ourselves that that second war was the climax and the vindication of the history of cinema.

3

What Are Brothers For?

ONE OF THE MOST disconcerting films about brothers ever made in America came from Warner Brothers. There is something indecent in its fable, it is so nakedly revealing of an eternal sibling hostility that responds to no moral code. And I am not surprised it came from Warners. Sibling rivalry was their thing.

The film is *East of Eden* (1955), drawn from the John Steinbeck novel, and before that from the mythic contest of the first two children on earth, Cain and Abel. In that Bible story, the two sons of Adam and Eve fall out, without any clear reason being offered. Is it that brothers are driven by nature to tend that way? The Lord looks upon Abel with respect, but he has no similar feeling for Cain, which prompted "wroth" in that brother, and then murder. Why is Cain regarded so unfairly? Just because he is not Abel?—or was God trying to be a scriptwriter?

When the director Elia Kazan proposed *East of Eden* to Jack

Warner as a film project, he found that Warner "hadn't read the book, didn't propose to, didn't even ask what it was about, and didn't ask whom I was going to cast. What he did ask was: 'What'll it cost?' 'About one six,' I said. 'You've got it,' he said. 'Cast who you want. Come and have lunch with me.'"[1]

If the picture had an agenda, that had more to do with Kazan's sense of himself as an ugly, resentful Anatolian life force determined to assert himself in America. If you read his great book, *A Life*, you can't help being thrilled by the chutzpah of Kazan against the world, and his frightening urge to betray others before they betrayed him.

In the Steinbeck novel, Charles and Adam Trask are deeply opposed half-brothers. They encounter a young woman, Cathy, who is as close to evil as Steinbeck or the American novel ever came. And Steinbeck was of German descent, Episcopalian. Cathy has killed her own parents and become a prostitute. The half-brothers rescue her, and Adam marries Cathy, without realizing that Charles has had her sexually. Cathy will give birth to twin sons, though the possibility is left hanging in the novel that the two sons come from the half-brothers.

Once she has delivered her twins, Cathy shoots Adam and leaves him with the new sons. Adam makes a ranch in Salinas, and Cathy goes away to Monterey. Those two places are only twenty miles apart, but in the biblical mood of the novel they are distant, so that Adam and his sons do not know that Cathy is alive still. Twinning in the novel is elemental and philosophical, and suited to the rivalry of brothers torn between some old order and new ways ahead. *East of Eden* may be the best Bible story Hollywood ever made, so compelling that it shrugs off any conventional attempt to be moral.

In the movie, Adam (Raymond Massey) has two sons who live with him on his farm in Salinas. They are named Aaron (Dick Davalos) and Cal (James Dean). Aaron is upright, handsome and polite to others; he is a good boy. But Cal is more crouched; he may be alluring, but he is not what movies of the early fifties called good-looking. He is shy, secretive, full of troubled thoughts; he feels wronged because there is a more trusting bond between his father and his brother than he can ever enjoy. In Dean's performance, Cal is the epitome of every bruised outsider kid in Warners history. His envy fixes on what seems like Adam's disapproving and withheld affection, and on the way a young woman, Abra (Julie Harris), is regarded as the natural fiancée for Aaron.

The narrative of the film (using a fraction of Steinbeck's story) has Cal farming beans to pay his father back the money lost on a pioneering refrigeration project. The bean business thrives as America's entry into the Great War comes closer. But when Aaron senses Cal's plan, he trumps his darker brother by giving their father a greater gift—news of his engagement to Abra. Adam rejects Cal's gift—of cash, $15,000, wrapped up as a birthday present—because Adam is agonized at being on the draft board, sending young men off to the war on which Cal is a profiteer.

The film is placed tenderly in the California of 1915–17, but it is myth and fairytale. In cruel revenge, Cal insists on taking Aaron to see their mother (Jo Van Fleet). She was thought to be dead, long ago, but in fact she keeps a brothel in Monterey. Aaron is so devastated he rushes off to enlist in the army. So Cal is left at home, to look after his invalid father (he has been shocked into a stroke), with Abra as his mate and beloved.

East of Eden is hideously unfair special pleading. Aaron is a prig, but no worse, and the action removes him from the arena, leaving the melancholy, self-centered Cal not just in charge but as the focus of attention. Dean's performance helped crystallize the new psychic yearning of teenagers as much as Elvis Presley would a year later. This rapturous male weepie is driven by the neediness of its director, Elia Kazan, a self-conscious outsider who sought revenge for himself.[2] Kazan was a magician with actors, and that shows in the stealthy, emerging feelings of James Dean. But I don't know another film anywhere that so directly understands the way one brother might need to vanquish the other. And the censors let it pass—but Warner Brothers had a good record at finessing censorship.

You can say this is mere coincidence and too little as a basis for any theory that might be applied to Warner Brothers, the company that insisted on sibling status in its very name. Still, Cain and Abel is the first murder story in the Bible, and this film came at a crucial moment in the story of Harry and Jack Warner.

East of Eden (which was very successful) could have come from other studios. But that is just a way of suggesting how so many movie stories have a persisting pattern of mythic emotional forces acting out family antagonisms. The Warner Brothers were like other studios in that instinct, but they did not want to escape a vein of fraternal opposition, the good and the bad working themselves out. *The Searchers* does not seem to be a Jewish film, but it begins in a smothered rivalry between brothers. More to the point (just because the antagonism is so much less emphatic), *The Jazz Singer* (the historic turning point for Warner Brothers) is about the struggle in one character to be both Jewish and American, a cantor's son and a sensational entertainer in vaudeville.

Not that all show business brothers were dogs prepared to fight. Joel and Ethan Coen have got on very well now for decades. George and Ira Gershwin are proverbial for the harmony of male siblings. The Epstein brothers, Philip and Julius, wrote together—they did a lot of *Casablanca* as a team, and that is a film in which ostensible rivals, Rick and Laszlo, become brothers in the fight for freedom, just as Rick and Louis Renault stroll off into the fog at "the start of a beautiful friendship."

On the other hand, Joseph L. Mankiewicz once told me that it was only possible to understand his life by grasping the ceaseless rivalry he had felt with his beloved brother Herman. David and Myron Selznick—producer and agent—were locked in a similar competition. Myron held on to a share of *Gone With the Wind* just to prove his brother had been a chump in selling out. Two sisters, Joan Fontaine and Olivia de Havilland, hardly liked to be reminded of each other.

You may say that these anecdotes are just natural struggles for power, comparable with feuds or skirmishes in any walk of life. After all, we may resent, rival, and hate the people we are related to (where else are we going to go?)—it's the same impulse that's involved in love. But the movie business of its own great days was uncommonly affected by these competitions just because they told the stories.

The family history of so many Jewish families who had come from eastern Europe to North America was confused, not always certain in the minds of the people themselves, and subject to the memory, the eloquence, or the scenario of elders. Jack didn't know the world that had produced him, or want to be tied to it. So the power to cast the story was vital, and subject to argument. Late in life, Jack Warner said he had forgotten what the family name had been. In 1965, he wrote, "I have never been to Poland. And it looks now as though I'll never go there."[3]

Of course, it wasn't even Poland. In the years that counted, this was Russia. But if you want to start the story, then you have to say that Benjamin Wonsal or Wonskolasor was living in Krasnoshilt or Krasnosielc in the middle of the nineteenth century. That was a village about fifty miles north of Warsaw. We learned to call it Poland after the Great War, but it had been part of the Russian Empire, and far more influenced by tsarist oppression. It was an area with a large Jewish population, and soon after German occupation in 1939 it would be the site of massacres at the hands of the Nazis just as it had been subject to Russian pogroms for several hundred years. It was a place where many people were in the clothing business. And where children got no official education and depended on family teaching.[4]

Little is certain, but Benjamin (born in 1857) lived with and was married to Pearl Leah Eichelbaum (born a year later), also from Krasnosielc. People married neighbors. He was apparently a shoemaker, though that does not mean he had no other occupations when need or opportunity arose. He and Pearl had children in Poland: a girl, Cecilia, the first, and dead at four; Moses, or Hirsch, or Hirz, born in 1881; Aaron in 1884; and Szmul in 1887. There was another son who died aged four, and another who made it to twenty. There would be five daughters, and if you think sons had to struggle, just imagine the girls, who were so much more thoroughly overlooked. But twelve children in all.

What happened next is subject to shipping lists and possible errors in the inventory of passengers. But it was common for the man to make such journeys first, with a wife and children coming on later. So it is said—with the energy of story attempting to settle confusion (and we must imagine this as the version told to young children)—that Benjamin sailed from Hamburg to Liverpool on the *Chester* in January 1888. Almost immediately, he took another ship from Liverpool to Baltimore. More than a year later, in October 1889, Pearl sailed from Bremen to Baltimore on the *Hermann*, with several children, including Moses, Aaron, and Szmul. The family was reunited, and it was around this time that Benjamin adopted the name Warner for all of them, and Moses became Harry, Aaron became Albert, and Szmul became Sam. Their ages in 1889 ranged from eight to two, so they can be forgiven for settling on one story or script that everyone could stick with. How do you tell a child his name has changed without setting free a kind of actor?

As the new Warner family made its way in North America, it rested for a time in Canada. Several other children were born (and survived), all girls except for Itzhak or Jacob, born in Ontario in 1892, and set to be Jack. So Jack was the North American boy, the kid, eleven years younger than Harry, and sooner or later not just the most inventive, ambitious, charismatic, and treacherous, but trouble. The family had spoken Yiddish. They had observed even if they had not directly suffered from Cossack cruelty. They had been so oppressed that they had sought to escape to the New World. That is part of the classic scenario of tales told to kids, and it surely had substance. But many who were poor and beaten did not risk wild dreams of something better. The Wonsals had been able to buy passage on ships for great voyages. They were never indigent. The real poor remained in eastern Europe, and in time, one way or another, they passed into the ground. But these guys became the Warner Brothers. In Youngstown, Ohio—one of the most dangerous places in America at that time—and then in Los Angeles, they made a point of sticking together.

Still, there would be those later who said Jack "killed" Harry. You don't have to credit that in an originalist sense of murder, but try forgetting it. Or see how far the Warner Brothers left alive in 1942–43 might look upon the lively melodrama of *Casablanca*, with its separated families, letters of transit, and noir dreams, as if they might be real. When Steinbeck finished *East of Eden*, he wrote to a friend with the realization, "Always I had this book waiting to be written." In rather the same way, though Jack Warner may never have read the novel, or intruded on the filming of *East of Eden*, it was as much his story as *The Jazz Singer*, *The Public Enemy*, *White Heat*, or so many of the family melodramas made under the Warner Bros colophon. Brothers cannot escape the need for battle.

By 1955, the year of *East of Eden*, the thing called Warner

Brothers was an immense success, and the kind of transformation that helped identify success in America. This was how showmakers out of Russia, without English, a name, or credentials, could become moguls in the land, as well as the arbiters who doled out fame to people named Cagney, Bogart, Davis, and Crawford. So long as you remembered the sardonic Hollywood principle: "It is not enough that I succeed—my best friend must fail."[5]

There's a boast in that candor—it's like the Clive James poem "The Book of My Best Friend Has Been Remaindered." But that at least admits an enemy. What emerges from decades of Warners pictures is the obsession with sibling rivalry and pals who become enemies. It's there in many big pictures discussed in this book, but there are so many more: *Four Daughters*, where the girls vie for the same guys; *The Hard Way*, a struggle between sisters; *Devotion*, with Ida Lupino as Emily Brontë, Olivia de Havilland as Charlotte, and Nancy Coleman as Anne; the deadly brothers in *Track of the Cat*; buddies fighting over a woman in *Other Men's Women*; family vendetta in *Pursued*; brothers split by a woman in *They Drive by Night*; co-workers in opposition in *Manpower*, on which Edward G. Robinson and George Raft came to blows; the brothers at odds in *The Master of Ballantrae*; and Bette Davis and Miriam Hopkins seething together in *Old Acquaintance* and *The Old Maid*, a natural extension of the actresses' real loathing for each other. You have to see how far the storytellers at Warners—the writers, the producers, the directors, and the actors—had this smell of intimate violence in their heads.

Harry and Jack Warner were always at odds, and that intensified as they became the decisive brothers. Harry was a self-conscious older brother, aware of the old country and of the codes the family needed to adhere to if they were to remain themselves during physical and social removal. Harry would like to think of himself as reasonable, good-natured, homely, and happy with that. Leo Rosten would say, "He was not an impressive man to meet. He led a brilliant business but he had no intention of being an outstanding personality. He was kind, honest, devout and devoted to family matters. He always observed the Jewish faith."[6] He was in the spirit of those actors who graced Warner Brothers movies for years—the friend, the sidekick, the amiable listener, the loyalist. You can see that impulse over the years in supporting actors like Alan Hale, Frank McHugh, Pat O'Brien, Jack Carson, Regis Toomey, George Tobias, and Ronald Reagan.

Jack may not have been a simple opposite to Harry, but he found himself in opposing him. He had no intention of being unimpressive. He worked hard to be better looking and to draw attention. People marveled at his bright teeth, and his habit of telephoning while sitting on the john. He adopted a thin mustache and snappy talk: if Warners led the way in bringing sound to the movies, why shouldn't Jack live up to that? He was a fair singer and a chronic teller of jokes, some of them in poor taste ("Uneasy lies the head that wears a toilet seat!"). Jack Benny said once, "Jack Warner would rather make a bad joke than a good picture."[7] Harry deplored the jokes and said they came from growing up in that racy Youngstown, Ohio, instead of in the shtetl. Of course, in many ways Harry was himself Americanized and a happy resident of fine American houses. But brothers thrive on their differences.

Jack was eager to be a show business person: this makes him awful in some ways, despised by many of his own employees. But he is irresistible, too, the showman in the family, the one who's likely to tell the world, "You ain't heard nothing yet!" He liked exclamation marks, while Harry found them vulgar. In 1907, Harry had married Rea Levinson, a longtime girlfriend. They had three children. The family lived according to the Jewish faith and tradition, and no one ever saw a sign that Harry needed to go outside his marriage for diversion. They were a steadfast and devoted couple, a model for the contented families that run through Hollywood movies.

But Jack Warner had seen another way. He was just twenty as the Warner Brothers moved into the picture business, and he quickly assessed the armies of pretty women dedicated to getting on screen by catching his eye. By 1915, Jack was in charge of the family movie exchange in San Francisco. That's where he met Irma Solomons, from a wealthy Jewish family. He wooed her and married her, and was educated and embarrassed by Irma's disdain for his own parents. As Neal Gabler puts it in *An Empire of Their Own*, Jack had "married up."[8] He and Irma had a single child, born in 1916, and Jack named the son Jack Jr., contrary to the Ashkenazi practice of not naming a child to honor a living relative. Harry deplored that decision, and he was shocked when Jack's marriage became a mask for affairs with actresses and women eager to be attached to the movies.

Harry had become a self-appointed guardian of family morals—it is the one sign of anything other than kindness in his life. His younger brother Sam had married the actress Lina Basquette in 1925. This was a shaming concession to the new world as Harry saw it. Lina was a Catholic, twenty years younger than Sam, with a reputation for fast living. Sam and Lina had a daughter, born in 1926, named Lita. But in 1927, when Sam died suddenly, Harry took steps to ensure that Lina would not have control of Lita, especially in the matter of religious upbringing. He went to law over it, and Lina yielded after Harry volunteered $300,000 as a trust fund for Lita. Thereafter, he and Rea were the child's legal guardians, despite repeated, failed attempts by Lina to regain custody.

Lina Basquette had a turbulent life. She returned to acting and worked in small parts until around 1940; she would be married eight times; she eventually retired to raise dogs in Pennsylvania. Great Danes. She never saw her daughter properly until the 1970s, and she was barred from any Warners inheritance. She died in 1994, hoping that her life story might be made into a movie.[9]

There was more. A young man named José Paige, from Albuquerque, New Mexico, was trying to make a career as a Latin lover actor named Don Alvarado. He actually made a few films for Warners, perhaps because of his young wife, Ann Boyar. She was sixteen when they married, a lustrous beauty, of Russian Jewish descent, and she caught Jack Warner's eye. He persuaded her to divorce Alvarado in Mexico, probably in 1933. Then Jack left his wife, Irma, and started living with Ann. They had a daughter, Barbara, in 1934, and in 1936 they were married.

Harry did not attend that ceremony. He wrote Jack saying that the only good thing about it was that their parents had not lived to see it.[10] They had died in 1934 and 1935. Harry regarded the divorce between Irma and Jack and the illegitimate child as a scandal and a disaster. It hardened a gulf between the brothers, just as it was a metaphor for the disquiet that the movies had made a cult of glamour and attractiveness, promiscuity and divorce.

Don Alvarado acted for a few years, but the field for Latin lovers was too crowded. He gave that up and became an assistant—at Warner Brothers (he knew people). As Don Page, he would be an assistant director on *East of Eden*.

Jack and Ann Warner, though frequently estranged, became a famous social couple in Hollywood, just as Harry shrank from any such attention. But the brothers were business partners nonetheless, and their business—with ups and downs—was an astonishing success. By the 1940s, Jack Warner had become Warner Brothers in the public eye, and he was more significant in running the studio than Harry. But Harry was president, still, strict, disapproving, and a mote and a beam in Jack's eye. "What a boring guy Harry was," said Darryl Zanuck once. "Jack was unreliable, but never boring."[11] In that passing remark lies a lesson of the picture business. Sooner or later, Harry had to go.

4

Family Dinner

IF IT WAS LATE 1903, or early 1904, Harry Warner was twenty-two; Abe was nineteen; Sam was sixteen; and Jack was eleven. It was dinner time at the Warner home in Youngstown, Ohio. You do not have to credit what follows in every detail, except that it is a story that was told by one of the family, years later, when that little girl had had the chance to hear versions of the evening told to her by many of the people who had been there.[1]

The family had tried Baltimore, Canada, Pittsburgh, and now Youngstown. Benjamin had kept working at shoe repairing, because in American cities looking for work and life the citizenry were soon wearing out their shoes. Harry had become an expert young cobbler. The family had had a flurry of activity with bicycles as the developing society sought technologies that might spare shoe leather. Their thoughts of business were all transport and friction. They had tried running a bowling alley, and they had spent time in the meat business, but shoes

37

were the standby because only the hopelessly poor went without them. The Warners were managing better than many families, but they were as yet unknown to anyone except themselves. Dinner was served and cleared away, and it was then that Pearl brought out her best latkes, with apple sauce and sour cream.

There were sisters in the group—Rose, Sadie, and Anna—and they were eager voices in the family, yet not much more important than two sisters who had died already in infancy. The light of the family and its hope were the brothers, and they had been taught by their parents and their own company to behave like a group. "One for all, and all for one," their father told them, though the Warners had few of the advantages of Dumas's musketeers.

But this was a special night—or so it would be memorialized—and Sam was the agent of the occasion. Sam then was the extrovert and the doer; he was the brother Jack looked up to. Somehow or other, for hard-earned money (perhaps as much as $1,000!), he had purchased one of the new kinetoscopes, a primitive movie projector, made by Thomas Edison, the marvels people were talking about, and Sam was proposing a movie show for the family on a white sheet he had pinned up on the wall.

It was Sam who had acquired the machine and heard about how it operated, because by consent he was the one in the family who had the best sense of how gadgets worked. So he had set up the projector and he had threaded it with the motion picture that came with it—for demonstration purposes—*The Great Train Robbery*, it was called.

At first, with whirring and clanking noises, a picture played on the sheet that seemed like life. But then the machine lost its sharp focus, and then it stopped. The miracle in those days had many mechanical impediments. So Sam was embarrassed, and he did what he could, with knives and forks from the dinner table, to get the machine to work. He knew that his father would be asking why it had cost so much if it wasn't working properly. Then the kid, Jack, leaped into the void, and proposed that, pretending to be the great and famous singer Leon Zuardo, he would now sing "Sweet Adeline." He gave out with that song and all the energy of a natural show-off reluctant to be subdued by the order and anxiety of his family. Brother Abe wondered aloud whether Sam had been conned by the neighbor who sold him the projector. Harry recalled that the neighbor had admitted it hardly ever worked without a problem.

But Sam, the machine, the miracle, and destiny would not be denied—all over the world, people were struggling to get these machines to work so that transport could be achieved without friction. Then, for eleven minutes or so, the assembled Warners watched *The Great Train Robbery*. Of course, it could have been any strip of film. But that's no reason not to note what a strange piece of work *The Great Train Robbery* was.

This was a Jewish family, from out of the shadow of Russia, lately installed in the United States. Most of them had not spoken English for their early years. They had had to learn and labor to find a place for themselves. They understood from the outset that many Americans feared or hated them because they were Jewish and foreign. They had recognized that in determining on a business, and a living for themselves, they would have to combat that. In settling for shoes, they realized that they would oppose the stereotype by which many Jews made basic items of clothing for people. They were resolved, if not desperate or anxious, to be respectable, law-abiding, and part of the new country.

Families of greater fortune or advantage tell themselves stories in which honesty, honor, hard work, and persistence are the most available of human assets. These are stories of virtue defended and rewarded by history. Not too far away, in Pitts-

burgh and then New York, a Lithuanian American, Lewis Selznick (Laiser Zeleznick, once), had read Dickens's *David Copperfield* to his son David, with that opening in which David
wonders whether he will be the hero of his own story. Thirty
years later, that David Selznick had produced a film from *David
Copperfield*, and it is still one of the most beloved movie versions of Dickens's work, with W. C. Fields as Mr. Micawber,
striving to make ends meet.

But *The Great Train Robbery*, directed by Edwin S. Porter
and made for the Edison Company, was a story in which sensation crowded out honor and respectability. Indeed, it is notable
that in the story of that dinner-table miracle, Ben or Pearl or
Harry did not remark on what a disgrace and a peril the film
was. But in the play of light and emulsion, motion and emotion,
something was slipping past all the safeguards of respectability.

It is the story of a band of robbers who hold up a train. It is
something we can now identify as a Western, shot in a mixture
of staged awkwardness and movie excitement. We see a gang of
robbers planning to waylay a locomotive. We see the local control office of the train, where a telegraph operation keeps track
of the action. We find ourselves on the train, with window rect-
angles of back projection giving the crude feeling of terrain
passing by. We see that operator beaten and tied up.

This is mundane and stilted, but then we are on the moving locomotive itself as the masked robbers seize control of the
train. They order it stopped. They separate the engine from
the body of the train. They call the passengers to assemble on
the track. When one of that group seeks to run away, a robber
shoots him down, and the splendid death fall leaves no doubt
about what has happened.

The plan to rob the train works—it becomes a "great" robbery, and then there is a screen event so lovely it may have made
people swoon in 1903. As the robbers escape and get away, so
the camera pans with their movement, celebrating it—motion

equals emotion (even Einstein could have guessed that, and in 1903 he was hot on the trail of relativity).

To this point, *The Great Train Robbery* could be a primer in how to take advantage of an innocent locomotive. A moment's reflection tells us that a motion picture business—which was only slowly emerging in 1903—could not leave the story at that. You could not make something that was so plainly "How to Rob a Train." The onus of business in America, or in any culture desiring respectability, was that the energy of the robbers had to be corrected and punished.

So it turns out. An inexplicable child revives and frees the operator. A telegraph message is sent. Very soon (this is only eleven minutes) a posse comes upon the robbers in the woods, dividing up their loot, and shoots them down. Fair's fair, you can say: you may have had the thrill of outlawry, but correction is guaranteed. Ben, Pearl, and Harry Warner could take some comfort in the show, even if that rascal Jack was jumping up and down with glee, riding a horse on the arm of the sofa, and firing off his fingers as six-guns.

Then something happens that is a prediction of the movies, Warner Brothers, and America. The story is done, but the movie continues with a head-on close-up of a Western character—a tough face with a cowboy hat and a drooping mustache, enough to make us think of photographs of the Wyatt Earp family (the Gunfight at the OK Corral in Tombstone was in 1881). This man then takes out his six-gun and fires six times into the camera, with smoke and flash at every shot, as if to say, "Take that, law and order!" (He actually keeps firing after the gun is empty.) We are still living with this uncanny, unexplored release of energy, will, and passion.

The traditional version of this Youngstown story comes from Cass Warner Sperling, a granddaughter of Harry Warner. And she wraps up the story in a way that indicates the influence of her grandfather and his sober sense of business. We are in no position now to decide whether the 1903 dinner scene happened exactly like this. But once the story was passed on, the facts ceased to matter too much:

> In the flickering light, Harry turned his face from the screen and watched the excited family audience as they viewed the magic shadows dancing on the sheet. *If this is what it does to my own brothers and sisters, and my parents, then think what it can do to others.* He imagined himself selling tickets to long lines of people waiting to see this new wonder on the wall come to life.[2]

The impact of *The Great Train Robbery* lingers still. It helps illuminate the ambiguity of two remarkable pictures, both of which were made for Warner Brothers.

The Letter was made in 1941, directed by William Wyler, from the Somerset Maugham play. The film starts at night, beneath a tropic moon, on a Malay rubber plantation. The camera tracks across the nocturnal scene until a shot rings out, and we come to the verandah of a wealthy house. The body of a man falls, and then we see the figure of a woman who has shot him. We know nothing beyond the fact of execution and the way this woman has carried it out, firing all six shots into the body of the man.[3]

It is something that she is Bette Davis, so clearly gripped by need and passion; and it is an addition that this woman has started off the picture by boldly shooting down a man as if given no other choice. Try to think of another woman in a picture (let alone a Warner Brothers movie) who had behaved with such fatal conviction. But it means a great deal to us, and our capacity for passion, that she has put all six shots into him, no matter that he is probably dead before number six.

In 1969, in *The Wild Bunch*, directed by Sam Peckinpah, and made in a state of barely controlled fury at his paymaster, Warner Brothers, there is a notable and more extended train robbery in which the iconography reminds one of the Edison-Porter film, just as it makes the wild bunch—outlaws, killers, destructive and self-destructive figures—the objects of our attention, our sympathy, and our wounded admiration. In fact, Peckinpah fought Warners over the gunfire. The studio sound department wanted to lay in standard library gun shots, but Peckinpah demanded that each firing be as fresh as a pretty girl just noticed.[4] *The Wild Bunch* is burning with the romance of fatalistic outlaws and unimpressed by law, order, or respectability. The railways are a toy trainset waiting to be plundered. And the gunfire is like glee and sex. No studio did more for gunplay and devil-may-care outlaws than Warners.

5

Mustache

You don't have to swallow every detail of that dinner-table story any more than you can scoff the latkes. It is a stretch to think that this far-from-secure family gave the teenage Sam $1,000 to buy that projector, even if within days they were cashing in by putting on screenings of *The Great Train Robbery* that took in several hundred dollars a week.[1] It's just as likely that Sam was shaky keeping the machine in working order; it's quite possible that a dozen other enterprises were horning in on the *Great Train Robbery* sensation; and it's probable that in Ohio and Pennsylvania, running those shows was subject to intimidating interference from gangs ready to smash your projector or from the agencies of the Edison corporation demanding to know where you had got their rights.

This was not a tidy, law-abiding business; it was a fierce competition making up its rules as it went along and always dreaming of California just to get away from gangs and copyright issuers on the East Coast.

Then consider that if the revelation at the dinner table occurred in 1903, it was twenty years before Warner Brothers were within sight of being established or secure. For many years, the family remained attached to shoes, bicycles, meat, and anything else that might put latkes on the table. It was only in 1923 that the name Warner Brothers appeared in legal documentation. If Harry really had that vision of how it was all going to turn out in 1903, we have to say that he was uncommonly patient or forgetful.

It wasn't until after the Great War that the four of them seemed to have had their picture taken. Moreover, it's worth adding that in 1917, when the United States entered the Great War, Harry was thirty-five, Albert was thirty-two, Sam was twenty-nine, and that kid Jack was twenty-four, ages at which service might have been taken for granted, especially for the Jack who later greeted the Second World War as a magnificent opportunity to be an honorary lieutenant colonel. (He had asked to be a general, but the authorities felt that was going too far.)[2] So it's not quite clear whether the Warner Brothers served in the Great War. Jack said that he and Sam went to an enlistment office only to be told they were too valuable doing their thing. So they were assigned to the Army Signal Corps, and that's how they did a film warning about syphilis.[3] As they worked on a movie intended for troops overseas, Sam observed that it might play very well at home, too.

Their later employee, Darryl Zanuck, was more active. He lied his way into the Nebraska National Guard at the age of fourteen and did brief service in France before the war ended. Not that the Warners ignored the war: they purchased the film rights to a successful and sensationalist book, *My Four Years in Germany*, and made it their first significant production.

But there are pictures of the brothers, from the early 1920s, a quartet lined up behind a shining desk in an empty room. They are joined by Harry Rapf, an early associate who would go on to be an important figure at Metro-Goldwyn-Mayer. But Rapf is short, slight, and insecure, which are terms that do not fit the brothers. They are the heroes or the founding fathers of this book, and it would be mean-spirited not to be impressed by the journey they made; still, one has to admit how far the four of them look like a tableau out of *The Godfather.*

These are big men, with an air of physical authority that adds to their unsmiling unison. Albert had been a football player, very solid, but trim and with an expression of unsentimental intent on his face. Albert handled a lot of the family business, the story goes, and he seems like no one you would think to mess with. As for Sam, he could be auditioning as muscle, protection, or even an enforcer. His face is set, gloomy, not as polished or urbane as Albert's. He looks like someone waiting for orders, and again he is no one to argue with. Harry is a little older, lighter, and more relaxed. But he keeps a straight, humorless gaze, as if he is resolved to give nothing away. At a glance you'd guess that Sam and Albert are waiting on Harry's orders, which are likely to be quiet, but effective.

Then there is Jack, the only one who is sitting less than upright, his head tilted over to one side. He is not smiling yet, but you feel he could, just as you wonder whether Sam and Albert have ever thought of smiling.

Now, you may say this analysis of a still photograph is less than fair, or like looking at movies. But there are other pictures of the brothers on their own that bear out this pattern. Sam and Albert do not smile. They stand still with their arms hanging at their sides. They do not seem to possess any kind of performing ease, let alone humor or appealing personality. A lot of people said Sam could be lively and funny, especially with women and gadgets. No one ever accused Albert of that. There is kindness sometimes, or philosophy, in Harry's face. But those three brothers keep their mouths closed. Gradually you begin to wonder whether it's because they never had their teeth fixed. It's then you realize that Jack grins a lot and flashes his teeth, which seem to be standard American cosmetics. It's there in the photographs, the promise that Jack was not just a clown, a singer, and a show-off, but a modern showman who was going to end up telling the family story and smiling at America.

Jack abandoned his own education for more pressing things before the age of twelve. Nor did the other brothers seem to pick up much schooling, so there are stories about the difficulty they had with reading. It is the general estimate that not one of them graduated high school. But Jack was the one of the four who wrote a book about himself—he called it *My First Hundred Years in Hollywood*—and it is cheerfully, flamboyantly unreliable, as well as co-written with Dean Jennings (who also wrote a book called *We Only Kill Each Other*, about Bugsy Siegel and his brotherhood).

In *My First Hundred Years*, amid its ragbag of scenes and scenario ideas, Jack reports a breakfast with his father in Pittsburgh. What are you going to have? asked Ben of the kid, and Jack replied that, if it was all right with Dad, he was going for ham and eggs, an American breakfast but not a family habit. Ben may have blinked. Then he said he'd have the same, country style. This is how Jack described that moment: "Our eyes met and we smiled, fellow schemers sharing a secret sin. I would never again be as close to him."[4]

Even if he'd had a slick ghost at hand, it is unbelievable that Harry would have written such a book, or recognized any need for it. But then you look at the pictures of Harry and you see, time and again, the upturned bow of his closed lips and their psychic reticence. Whereas the young Jack is itching to grin, to break out of the behavioral models Harry believed in. In the same way, he let his first marriage go to hell and lived with his mistress in ways that shocked his sisters, and the forbiddingly respectable Harry.

That public affair took off in the early thirties, and it seemed to be in the line of Jack's several previous romances with actresses. He had had an affair with the Broadway singer and dancer Marilyn Miller, once the mistress of Florenz Ziegfeld and the wife of Jack Pickford. Warner was so keen on her that he promoted a 1929 hit for Warners, the fourth all-talking picture, *Sally*, taken from her 1920 hit show written by Jerome Kern for Ziegfeld. More than his brothers ever dared, Jack had pursued his chances with pretty women in pictures as an obvious fruit of the profession. But with Ann Alvarado he moved on into a real show business display, where the affair became a daring, naughty asset, even a status symbol.

As Jack and other Hollywood moguls saw it, taking advantage of the pretty women applying to the picture business was obvious, expected. This is the most direct conflict that existed between Harry and Jack, the old sense of family honor and the undeniable insight that movies were selling sex.

Jack kept no record of his automatic conquests or the afternoon visitors to his office. But the habit was known, and it's built in to the theory of movies as an arena for sexual fantasy. Sometimes fiction captures the dynamic more clearly than rumor. In Norman Mailer's novel *The Deer Park*, set in Hollywood, there is a studio head, Herman Teppis, who has girls come to his office to service him. One woman arrives and repeats what an executive has told her, that "I should do what you wanted, Mr. Teppis."

What he wants is to be fellated, in what is a discreet description (though Mailer's novel upset people in 1955, and changed publishers). What follows the deed is most interesting. The girl departs, and Teppis returns to business—he has a conference coming up on a picture called *Song of the Heart*. But then Mailer gives us a glimpse of the tyranny and even the vengeance that reside in power: "Teppis ground out his cigar. 'There's a monster in the human heart,' he said aloud to the empty room. And to himself he whispered, like a bitter old woman, close to tears, 'They deserve it, they deserve every last thing that they get.' "[5]

At the same time, Jack did something his brothers had never thought of. He grew a pencil mustache, a hard line that would need daily attention, and the italic overlining for his smile. You can say that was chance. But there's a pattern. Darryl Zanuck joined Warners in the twenties and helped introduce a kind of emphatic storytelling that would become the character of the studio, but when he started out, the nervous Zanuck pitched a story for Rin Tin Tin on all fours, acting out the part of the dog. Jack responded: "Kid, go buy some glasses and grow a mustache. You'll look older. Oh yeah, I like your story. We'll film it."[6]

When Jack first saw Clark Gable in *It Happened One Night*, he wrote to his new executive, Hal Wallis (the man who had replaced Zanuck), "I think we should definitely have Lyle Talbot grow a mustache just like his. It gives him a sort of a flash and good looks."[7]

This transformation never really worked for Talbot, but the thin black line and the hope for flash was the marker for Jack Warner. A few years later, a crucial decision was made with Errol Flynn—he should grow a mustache, and then it should be made darker. Jack grinned, for now Flynn looked like him, the *shvontz*.[8]

6

For Liberty?

IN HINDSIGHT, in his own book, Jack did muse over the slow development of Warner Bros. In many parts of the East and the Midwest, the brothers were doing worthwhile business, playing pictures in parlors, halls, and any enterprise with a big room. But there was "a lack of pictures." Throughout the emerging business, geniuses were discovering that as well as a projector and a room you needed a movie. So make them yourself: that's what motivated the new businesses that had become Paramount, MGM, Universal, and Fox before the name Warners was known.

In New Castle, Pennsylvania, the boys found a funeral parlor available for screenings. It even had its own chairs and an undertaker who said he was ready to delay a funeral so long as a good picture was playing.

By 1915, the brothers had several film exchanges, clearing-house facilities where local exhibitors could rent movies made by other companies. It seems that that exchange business had its ups and downs, so that the brothers were unable to get properly established or to pursue stray thoughts of actually making films. That's why *My Four Years in Germany* is so essential in the Warners legend, even, as Neal Gabler observed, as important as *The Birth of a Nation* was to Louis B. Mayer: Mayer had the New England distribution rights to Griffith's movie, and he made so much money from it that he soon ventured into production.[1]

James W. Gerard (1867–1951) was a lawyer who had served on the New York Supreme Court from 1907 to 1911. In 1913, he was appointed by President Woodrow Wilson to be ambassador to Germany. In that position, Gerard became a spokesman in Berlin for several Allied causes, including the neutrality or not of Belgium, the "crime" of German submarine warfare, and the matter of German atrocities during the war. When diplomatic relations between the United States and Germany were broken off in February 1917, Gerard returned to America and wrote a memoir, *My Four Years in Germany*, which became a best-selling book.

The fever of war had seized filmmaking, so it is not surprising that Lewis Selznick and William Fox, at least, were also inquiring about the film rights to Gerard's book, which was a close account of the ambassador's dealings with Kaiser Wilhelm and other German officials. Fox was reputed to have offered $75,000 for the movie rights.

Yet the legend goes that Sam Warner, who was barely educated, came upon the book in a Los Angeles store. He started to read and was only halfway through when he telephoned Harry in New York and said this was the movie they needed to make. Harry liked the plan, but was low on funds. So they cabled Gerard and fixed a meeting at which Harry hit the right high-minded note: "Mr. Ambassador, film is the great founder of peace. When people understand each other, they need not fight. I feel it is our patriotic duty to thousands of Americans who cannot read to make a motion picture of your book."[2]

Apparently Gerard was impressed by Harry's sincerity, even though he had already received a $75,000 check from Fox. Instead of cashing it, Gerard said he would wait to see Warners' plan for a script—after all, the book was a study in diplomacy. Gerard actually doubted that all his detailed and frustrating meetings could make an exciting film. Again, Harry had a sermon ready: "Ambassador, the movie I make can carry to the American people and the world, your stirring warning about the menace of the German military threat. The picture will help arouse the world at large as to why we must fight for civilization."[3] As even Jack admitted, the sober Harry "could have sold swimsuits to a South Seas tribe."[4]

Still, when Gerard said he was listening, and open to an offer, Harry had only $2,000 on hand. But he offered $50,000 plus twenty percent of the profits. The uplifting story says that Gerard agreed, that Harry went out and did raise the full amount (it seems that Mark Dintenfass was a helper), that the picture was made and grossed between $800,000 and as much as $1.5 million in 1918 (the reports vary), leaving $130,000 in clear profit for the Warners. Thus *My Four Years in Germany* is hailed as the decisive start of Warner Brothers as a movie-making operation.

But if that were so, you'd expect the Warner Brothers name to be all over the picture. Which is not the case. The film announces itself as a production of My Four Years in Germany Inc., as directed by William Nigh. The insignia on the titles is not WB but WN. Nowhere does the proud name Warner appear. Yet the picture is more than one hundred minutes long and, within the bounds of naïve propaganda and halting narrative techniques, it is something to see.

The script is credited to Charles Logue, and there are suggestions that he worked on it with Harry Warner. Like William Nigh, Logue was at the start of a solid career on undistinguished pictures. The titles to the movie quote freely from Gerard's book, and they are unashamed about the propaganda purpose of the enterprise. The film depicts the kaiser and his supporters as creatures from wicked melodrama—not too far from the satirical depiction of the bosses in Eisenstein's 1925 film *Strike*—and the action reports shocking behavior from German troops, and events that the ambassador never witnessed. So the moral purpose of the film is sacrificed to inflammatory (and unsubstantiated) scenes of war's horror. The repeated claim that "facts" are being shown is a travesty of any careful historical approach. As early as possible in film history, this is "a war movie" of a kind that Warners would return to with mixed motives in *Sergeant York; Air Force; Objective, Burma!;* and even *The Green Berets*, the John Wayne Vietnam picture from 1968 that Warners would release, for they liked to please Wayne as often as possible.

So the Germans in *My Four Years* massacre prisoners, they round up Belgian women with clear prospects of rape, they abuse victims of typhus. They behave like "Huns," or in the way Germans were demonized in so much fiction of the era. At the very end, as American troops arrive, they bayonet German soldiers with a zest that the audience has no way of resisting. A war movie is action, danger, and bloodshed, predicated on our winning.

That approach was standard in fictions of the Great War— it is not so different from the attitudes in *Hearts of the World*, Griffith's film of 1918, though Griffith was a more sophisticated storyteller. But *My Four Years* has real scale and production values. Somehow, this scatterbrained project has stumbled into a great wardrobe of military uniforms. There are exterior scenes of troop movements (some of them in snow). There are even scenes of some large fleet, with shots taken from the deck of a battleship at sea—they go rather nicely with one spark of mocking humor, where Admiral von Tirpitz is seen playing with toy ships in a nursery pool of water. One can understand how, in 1918, an audience was impressed enough to produce something like the claimed gross income.

The interiors (allegedly shot in a Biograph studio in the Bronx) have dark backgrounds that economize on sets and furniture, but the splendid uniforms are a diversion, and the acting is within the range that was tolerated at that time. Halbert Brown is impressively restrained as Gerard, and Louis Dean is suitably odious as the kaiser. There is little human subtlety on display, and no dramatic understanding of the role it might have in a crude silent movie. (Though, granted the years between, the view of Renault and Strasser in *Casablanca* is not really so advanced or deepened.) But the film still plays as an historic curiosity, and it does not feel like beginners' luck.

The film was certainly noticed, but it would be another five years before Warner Brothers had their name on a movie that might match this. There is a sequel noted in some of the flimsy records (it does not seem to exist as anything to be seen), called *Beware!* (also known as *Germany on Trial*), in which Gerard warns of the abiding dangers of Germany. (Don't forget, this man lived long enough to see Anschluss, Auschwitz, and *The Big Sleep*.) Logue and Nigh apparently worked on the follow-up, and that film is said to be a Warners production. That was nearly a hundred years ago, and we don't know enough about the actual work done. We never will—even if anything about the picture business had taught us to trust credits.

My Four Years in Germany was an awful, ambitious picture, stupid and noisy as only silent pictures could be, high-minded and low-down, too long yet too short (it assesses the war in 108 minutes), but it was carried all the way to the precious screen. Certainly the Warners were involved on it, and the film can be seen still. But it was actually distributed by First National, and not by a series of exchanges belonging to Warner Brothers.

First National was an amalgamation of theatre chains, begun in 1917, that became a distribution company and then a production studio in its own right. In 1928, it would be taken over by Warners, a sign of how rapidly the brothers had started to develop by the late twenties.

But that was not yet, and it was before the dog.

7

Rinty

WHEN IT COMES TO a straightforward chronicle of Warner Brothers and its advance on fame and glory, you may well sigh at reaching 1920 and say, well, really you haven't heard anything yet—or not nearly enough. So stay open to at least a dash of the unexpected. If I were to say that in the rough-and-tumble of the motion picture business before 1920, the Warner boys had let time pass them by, you could hardly argue. All too many short-lived film enterprises had been launched in those years on a press handout and an uncertain piece of machinery—and perished.

The Warners were all for one, and one for all (at least in Harry's mind), but they hadn't made a mark beyond dithering about in the business, thinking of buying theatres and film exchanges, and getting used to calling themselves Warner. I don't want to be unkind to them (there were so many others in the same business who could do that with more bite and accuracy), but even their famous breakthrough, *My Four Years in Germany*, is not what the books say it is, and not something you really wish to spend the 108 minutes watching.

You could have written them off, as many of their rivals must have done. More or less, they'd been knocking their heads against the wall for twenty years without even getting their name on their one hit film. So perhaps they made a little money out of the film, in an age when a little went a long way, especially if you had never given up on shoes, meat, soap, or bowling alleys.

Nothing but a sense of wonder will carry us from the embarrassing pomp of *My Four Years in Germany* to the way, in just a few years, Warners made it to the big show, this low-down, stumbling outfit that somehow blundered into an unlikely trifecta—Ernst Lubitsch, John Barrymore, and a charming German shepherd—and then capped it off with an invention they hardly understood. What explains this upheaval of luck? Maybe it was Darryl Zanuck.

While still in the military, Zanuck had been writing lively, imaginative letters home to his grandfather about being in Belgium as the war ended. No one said the letters were models of fact or modesty—what does a grandfather expect? But an officer saw some of them and got them published in *Stars and Stripes*. The idea of being a writer germinated in the furiously ambitious kid (he was still only eighteen), and after a few days in the Midwest he moved himself out to California. A director, Frank Lloyd, saw him on the street—handsome, short but pale—and asked him to test for the lead in a film of *Oliver Twist* (Jackie Coogan got the part).[1]

In the next few years, Zanuck did everything and anything he had to—his industry is in marked contrast with the languid Warner brothers. Zanuck boxed a little; he was a riveter in a shipyard; he exulted in his physical prowess; and he wrote. An obvious target for that enterprise was the movie business, with its relentless need for story. There is even a legend that the young Zanuck sought an interview with Jack Warner and was turned away because Jack was "busy." So Darryl thought he would write a book. To that end, he persuaded one of his employers—Yuccatone Hair Restorer—to have him write a story that was also an advertisement for Yuccatone. Product placement began early, and Zanuck came up with the selling line, "You've Never Seen a Bald-Headed Indian."[2]

And so Zanuck became a published author, in 1923—*Habit: A Thrilling Yarn Where Fiction Ends and Life Begins*. I am not making this up—even if he was. As a Zanuck biographer, Mel Gussow, would write, with appealing restraint: "In these stories life ends and fiction begins. All are concerned with the moral regeneration of people corrupted by 'liquor, hop and women.' Actually the degradation is far more exciting and even appealing than the regeneration, which must say something about Zanuck's divided allegiances in matters of morality."[3]

Here is the spirit of *My Four Years in Germany*: a vein of preaching that somehow strays into the lurid bad things people do. We are getting closer to a model for the gangster pictures that Zanuck would do so much to launch.

Habit the book vanished, not helped by the discovery that bottles of Yuccatone were beginning to explode in customers' bathrooms—largely because the product was actually a cover for alcohol. It was at about this time, in his pursuit of fitness, that Zanuck sought to join the Los Angeles Athletic Club. He was declined, and when he asked his grandfather how this could be, the report came back that the club believed Zanuck was Jewish.

Undaunted, and unceasingly athletic in body and spirit, he pushed his way into writing episodes for run-of-the-mill movie serials—notably *The Telephone Girl* and *The Leatherpushers*. Some remarked that in the material he wrote, Zanuck sometimes copied himself, or other stories he had read. But the movie business was already a duplicating machine in which there were few unique narrative structures. Zanuck pushed them out as fast as he could type. If you were making a movie of this life of his— and why not, didn't he deserve it?—you could cut from a photograph of Zanuck at his typewriter, surrounded by scripts, to one of a German shepherd dog gazing down at the keyboard. The two were made for each other, and together they would alter the status of Warners in Hollywood.

Corporal Lee Duncan had found his Rinty in France, though this dog was probably being trained for the German army. Duncan had cared for two lost puppies and brought them home. He had become attached to his dog, and seen intense character and physical prowess combined in the animal. He saw a hero. Then at a dog show in California, Rinty jumped a wall that was nearly twelve feet high, and a friend had filmed the leap. It wasn't just a dog doing a dog thing, it was an event on film, a heroic vault and a scene. Duncan sent the film clip to a newsreel company on spec, and one day a check for $350 came back. This heroism was negotiable. Strangers would buy it, just to marvel at the grace and the surprise.

There were other such heroes in films: there was a dog called Strongheart, and most cowboy heroes had horses with names. We easily find Rin Tin Tin comic, or charming, but that loses sight of his nobility on film, just as it risks forgetting how far film was waiting to achieve that trick with any image, animal or human. As Susan Orlean puts it in her book *Rin Tin Tin: The Life and the Legend*:

> Dogs, in fact, were perfect heroes: unknowable but accessible, driven but egoless, strong but tragic, limited by their muteness and animal vulnerability. Humans played heroes in films, too, but they were more complicated to admire because they were so particular—too much like us or too much unlike us or too much like someone we knew. Dogs, on the other hand, have the talent of seeming to care and understand

about humans in spite of not being human and perhaps are better at it because of that difference. They are compassionate without being competitive, and there is nothing in their valor that threatens us, no demand for reciprocity. As [Duncan] knew very well, a dog could make you feel complete without ever expecting much in return.[4]

A dog in a silent film needed no intertitles, not just because he said nothing but because his entire being was so fully expressed and removed from the unfathomability available to us in life, but so often missing from silent pictures. Its poetry was in having nothing to say. A dog in silent motion was a hymn to the brimming emotional simplicity that urged it along.

This is going beyond what the Warners or Zanuck felt, but it is also on the brink of identifying the phenomenal achievement of sound. Rin Tin Tin established the clumsy, awkward studio held back by lack of enterprise or instinct. Jack Warner called the dog "the mortgage lifter." The studio paid him $1,000 a week on top of what it paid Duncan as a trainer—and the dog never complained or got a lawyer or an agent in the way Jimmy Cagney or Bette Davis would in just a few years. Greta Garbo asked to have a puppy. Zanuck took one himself, if only to be obliging. Warners soon had thousands of requests for pictures of Rinty signed with a paw print and a written line from Lee Duncan, "Most faithfully yours, Rin Tin Tin."[5]

The first Rinty film was *Where the North Begins*. Duncan had submitted a crude script, and footage of the dog's great jump. Harry Warner said, why not? Harry Rapf was put in charge. The film was so cheap to make at an hour and it grossed over $300,000 in a weekend. That's when Zanuck appeared, as the writer for more Rinty films—notably *Find Your Man* and *Lighthouse by the Sea*. The films built amazingly. Rinty and Duncan went on a tour of public appearances, and soon Zanuck was supervising his pictures. This was 1923 to 1925. There would be twenty-seven of the films, before sound and old age killed

Rinty off. Along the way, there was a big write-in vote for the dog getting the first acting Oscar. But the humorless Academy was set on respectability. They foresaw a bad precedent and gave the prize to Emil Jannings instead, an actor who couldn't wag his tail without labored forethought.

8

Mama, Darlin'

OCTOBER 6, 1927, at the Warner Theatre on Broadway at 52nd Street—it was a Thursday—is a turning point in motion picture history, the moment at which a raw display of mime, archaic sentiment, pretensions of Art, and a lantern show turned into a complete illusion that would release the fantasy that has altered our ideas about ourselves. That October 6 surpasses the opening of *The Birth of a Nation* or *Gone With the Wind*. It is when B.C. becomes A.D. It is also when something Jewish passes into the American bloodstream and dissolves, as if recognizing that it can't be just "Jewish" anymore.

With that burden of cultural history, it mattered not at all that the picture opening that night—*The Jazz Singer*—was pretty bad. Its import was clearer that way. The lesson had to be learned, that the technology was more important than its messages. Never mind the faithful agility of Rin Tin Tin, the sultry self-mockery of John Barrymore, or the passing wit of

Ernst Lubitsch; sound was what made Warner Brothers and how they transformed an understanding of understanding as surely as if they had been Freud or Einstein. So it's a nice irony that not one of the brothers was present that evening.

Only three of them could have made the opening of the picture, but they were elsewhere. Harry, Albert, and Jack were at Sam's funeral, in Los Angeles. The doctors at the California Lutheran Hospital ascribed the death to pneumonia, but Jack Warner had no doubt—"*The Jazz Singer* killed him," because of the way Sam had been in charge of that production and its struggle toward synchronized sound.[1]

Late in September, when Sam had thought of taking the train east for the New York première, he had been short of energy and complaining of terrible headaches. Jack was worried (he wrote later): "Sam looked wan and listless. I knew he had worked day and night for weeks, losing weight and deepening the hollows under his eyes."[2] Sam was unsteady on his feet at times. *The Jazz Singer* had taken an enormous effort—though it's not clear how much of the technical detail Sam understood. But not understanding machinery can wear you out. Nor is it certain that Jack was there to see the hollows under Sam's eyes.

The doctors determined that Sam had several badly infected teeth. He had tried to have them extracted at the dentist's, but complications had set in, and he was taken into hospital. There was talk of an acute mastoid infection and a cerebral hemorrhage. He had several operations. Albert was at his bedside, with Sam's wife, Lina. Harry and Jack were hurrying to California by train. Sam died at 3:22 a.m. on October 5, a matter of hours before *The Jazz Singer* was set to open. In that movie, the father, the cantor expires once he has heard his once-lost son, Jackie, return to sing Kol Nidre on Yom Kippur. The tangle of fact and fiction is uncanny, but most of the moguls felt their life was a movie.

Every folkloric cliché about sound's role in silent cinema is justified. For twenty years, audiences had shouted out what they thought characters were saying. Anything from a piano player to a full orchestra provided live accompaniment to a film, and the audience was ready to add sound effects: a "bang!" for a shot, plaintive weeping for sorrow, and feet drumming on the theatre floor for scenes of pursuit. But those sounds were labored and physically produced. Above and beyond that, there lay the possibility of magical sound, accompaniment that needed no effort, and had the fluency of the picture.

When sound came to the movies, it was in a rush, as if nothing mattered more than audience excitement. There was also a laborious technological revolution, and that led to radical alterations in the business of film and its quality as a fantasy narrative. Credit has to go to Sam Warner and to a couple of technicians he had working for him. Some goes to Darryl Zanuck, the most acute showman involved on *The Jazz Singer.* Still, it's hard to envisage the change without the panache of a performer, Al Jolson. For the public, the inventive process didn't matter—it was Jolson giving utterance. It was his mouth.

On April 25, 1917, a young man just out of the University of Illinois, Samson Raphaelson, went to see the musical *Robinson Crusoe, Jr.*[3] It starred Al Jolson, as a dreaming chauffeur, done in blackface. Jolson was Jewish, born in Sprednik, Lithuania, as Asa Yoelson, and arriving in America when he was eight. Jolson never knew his birthdate for sure, and he was probably a few years older than he admitted. But he had become the outstanding performer on Broadway, a singer with pathos and zest in his voice, a dynamo of sentiment and sympathy, with large begging eyes in a face and a head that seemed to grow larger as his hair receded.

Jolson specialized in blackface routines, and he was surely drawn to the emotional appeal of black blues singers. He was even called "a jazz singer," but that was in an age when few people had much understanding of jazz, or how it expressed black

experience. How many white people believed blacks had experience? So Jolson traded on an archetype that is offensive today,
and which makes *The Jazz Singer* nearly as hard to stomach as
The Birth of a Nation.

Raphaelson was bowled over by Jolson in *Robinson Crusoe,
Jr.*—"I shall never forget the first five minutes of Jolson—his
velocity. The amazing fluidity with which he shifted from tremendous absorption in his audience to a tremendous absorption in his song."[4] Raphaelson felt that the jazz singer Jolson
was playing had the dramatic passion of a Jewish cantor, and
that was close to the dynamic in Jolson's American career as
a young man. The son of a cantor, Al had gone show business
(against his father's wishes) to the point of being the top star in
variety. As movies soared as a trade, Jolson was a model for the
Jewish impulse celebrated by show business and a heroic figure
to George Gershwin and Irving Berlin, as well as the Warner
brothers. In his intense being and his need for attention and
command, Jolson personified Jewish storytelling for a universal
audience. You can't see Barbra Streisand in *Yentl* without feeling Jolson's heritage.

Raphaelson was so moved that he wrote a short story, "Day
of Atonement," about a character torn between the synagogue
and Broadway. And then nearly a decade later he turned that
into a play, *The Jazz Singer,* that opened on Broadway in September 1925, with George Jessel as Jackie Rabinowitz who becomes Jack Robin, a star on Broadway, and who goes home to
sing Kol Nidre for his dying father, a cantor—*and resolves to give
up show business.* The play was straight melodrama; the singing
it required was all heard offstage. Harry Warner was moved by
the play, and he bought the film rights fast for $50,000, agree-
ing to pay Jessel thirty thousand to repeat his performance on
screen. Harry was heard to tell the actor, "It will be a good picture to make for the sake of racial tolerance, if nothing else."[5]
But Harry saw this as just a silent movie.

In those mid-1920s, Warners was not yet in the first rank of movie studios, though it was getting there, thanks to the Lubitsch comedies, the unpredictable arrangement with John Barrymore, and that steadfast Rin Tin Tin. There are claims, from competing sources, that Warners was flourishing yet often on the point of collapse—chances are both stories had substance, varying from week to week, or day to day.

The Lubitsch films—*Kiss Me Again* (1925), *Lady Windermere's Fan* (1925), *So This Is Paris* (1926)—were sophisticated and even exquisite comedies that did poor business. Lubitsch knew this, and wanted out; he telegraphed Harry, "You have always been complaining of being unable to make money with my pictures. And my own earnings certainly far below amount I could get everywhere else. Am very skeptical regarding your plans of bigger pictures because they require different facilities and acting material from what you have. Fully realize what world expects from me and therefore repeat proposal of separating after next picture."[6]

That was January 1926, when Harry was telling Jack (who was trying to act for Lubitsch) that *Kiss Me Again* never managed to play longer than three days in one venue. "His pictures are over people's heads," said Harry. He told Lubitsch his pictures were "too subtle. . . . The world wants thrills and excitement."[7] Soon Lubitsch would be at Paramount, a more suitable home, because his touch was appreciated there, and because Paramount had distribution resources and theatres that surpassed anything at Warners.

Sam and Jack together had persuaded Harry to offer John Barrymore a contract—for $75,000 a picture—on the grounds that so handsome and distinguished a reputation was bound to work on film. Harry had been dubious: he had heard that Barrymore was a womanizer and a drunk, as well as an actor who tended to pose and offer his celebrated profile to the movie camera. But Barrymore came to Warners for *Beau Brummel* (1924),

The Sea Beast (a version of *Moby-Dick*, 1926), and *Don Juan* (1926). The latter had been most interesting because it was a film that came with a synchronized sound track—though only music. There were also more than a hundred kisses in the film, as Barrymore wooed characters played by Estelle Taylor and Mary Astor (his former lover, discovered for *Beau Brummel*, but then cast aside in favor of Dolores Costello).[8]

This gesture towards sound was the product of Sam's enthusiasm. It was he who had attended demonstrations at Western Electric's Bell Laboratories, and been struck by the authenticity of sound effects. He had persuaded Harry and the others to look at the tests that involved a synchronized sound-on-disk system. Harry (the decisive figure still) had been unimpressed, except in the matter of musical accompaniment. Nagged by Sam, he had agreed to *Don Juan* having music. As for talk, he thought that was unnecessary, pedestrian, and contrary to the spirit of movies.

Don Juan opened on August 6, 1926, in New York, with the disk system as perfected by Vitaphone. It's fascinating to see how far Harry and Warners as a whole were at cross purposes. They had a new gimmick at the very least, and they had spent nearly $800,000 on *Don Juan*. Harry himself organized a big opening. The Warner Theatre at Broadway and 52nd was then the only place equipped for Vitaphone. So Harry telephoned Will Hays, once postmaster general, now head of the Motion Picture Producers and Distributors of America, and soon to devise a censorship code for movies. He asked Hays to do a short introductory speech on Vitaphone. Hays remembered it as 325 words. He wrote the speech and rehearsed it. He had the text written up on cards and put on an easel. "In the recording room that evening I stood in front of a microphone and a camera and said my piece—with gestures." Hays attended the première and observed that he "didn't set the world on fire."[9] But suppose Barrymore had talked, and kissed, and sighed.

When he wrote his memoir, Hays recalled a Dallas newspaper that had heard and guessed at the truth: "Nothing has happened in New York this summer which is more important for Dallas than the opening of the New Warner Motion Picture Theatre. It means that before long the greatest artists will be available to the remotest villager, in a form so lifelike that the very personality of the artist seems to be present, and it is easier than not to believe he is actually before you."[10] Silent pictures were about icons; sound delivered actual, impulsive humanity.

In the months that followed *Don Juan* (it was only a modest hit), Sam had a brainwave to urge on his brothers. If a project was called *The Jazz Singer*, and if it was about music, why let it stay a silent picture? Suppose Jackie/Jack would sing. What happened next comes to us from Jack Warner as a fast-talking dialogue scene of a kind that was still a few years away at Warner Brothers. But it plays, and Jack's version makes him central, even if Harry was still leader.

The studio is about to put *The Jazz Singer* into production. So Jack calls George Jessel, the attached actor, about a start date. Jessel points out that his original contract had said nothing about singing. Jessel could sing, but with no special dramatic urgency.

"I guess I don't like your attitude," says Jack. "You want more money, right? How much?"

"I want ten grand more," Jessel tells him.

"You've got it. Come on out and I'll give you a binding letter."

"The letter first, then I come out," says Jessel.

"Goddammit it, Georgie. I give you my word."

"That's not enough. Your brother Harry will never go for the deal."

"Okay, Georgie. If you can't take my word let's forget the whole thing."

"All right, the deal's off," says Jessel. He had been a big-

timer once, but he was walking into his closet in history.[11] He
would add later that he was offended by the way the movie
changed the play by having Jackie sing Kol Nidre and then go
back to show business. Having your matzo and eating it.

In his book, Jack says he asked himself, "Now what the hell
do I do?" at Jessel's departure. But maybe he had a hunch. He
went to Eddie Cantor, who told him, nicely, that he'd rather
not betray Jessel. So then Jack thought of Jolson—"He had the
sob in his voice" and was less sensitive to betrayal. Jack sent
Morrie Safier, an executive, to find Jolson, who was playing in
Denver. In an hour the deal was done: seventy-five thousand,
with a third up front in cash. The contract was signed May 27,
1927. That famous opening was less than five months away.
Years later, Jessel would say that he believed Jolson had contributed money towards *The Jazz Singer* budget to secure the
part. Yet the picture cost less than half the amount of *Don Juan*

The Jazz Singer is so archaically sentimental, and pious towards its sentimentality, that it seems to come from the nineteenth century—yet sometimes so alive, naked, and exhilarated
that it can leave you wanting to make a new movie yourself.
God knows what Harry Warner thought it might do for race
relations. Did he really believe this epic schmaltz would make
Jewish culture more acceptable? Did he fail to see the injury
done to black people, and the travesty made of "jazz"? *The Jazz
Singer* is a helpless admission of the existential distress felt by
European Jews trying to assimilate in America. No one knew
that passage better than Al Jolson, whose father despised Al's
show business glory. Al's brother Harry would say, "The chief
difficulty in our home life was that Al and I had been absorbed
by American customs, American freedom of thought, and the
American way of life. My father still dwelt in the consciousness
of the strict, orthodox teachings and customs of the old world."[12]
Who else should play the part?

And so the painful story seeps its way from the screen, so slowly as to make an extra marvel of sound when it comes. Melodramatically, this is still a silent film—so when the father (played by Warner Oland, the Swedish actor who would later play Charlie Chan) whips his son Jackie for singing at the local beer hall, there is no sound of the whip or pained cries from behind the closed door. But the boy, rather well played by Bobby Gordon—who really could be a kid Jolson, with staring eyes and looming head—says he will run away to the world of jazz, beer halls, and show business. The father tells the mother that they have lost their son—and many families were split apart on dilemmas like those of the Rabinowitzes. The broken family thrives in the movies: it is there in *Symphony of Six Million*, one of the classic films about Jewish assimilation in America; it can even be felt at the heart of *The Godfather*, an epic on the old ways and the new (where one brother has another killed at the close of *Part II*).

When Jack's real life is made clear, the father is stopped in his tracks. He falls ill, as if stricken—this is like the collapse of Raymond Massey's father in *East of Eden*. But show business can handle death, like a gambler palming a card. The insolent compromise of *The Jazz Singer* is that Jack's demanding Broadway show is canceled for only one night; the errant son can go home to sing Kol Nidre so that his father passes away in peace (and it *is* Jolson singing the sacred song). And then next night, there he is, back on stage with "Mammy" and the other songs that besmirch real jazz. The solution to the drama was to have it both ways, to get both big scenes on the same plate, to be pious while making a killing. At that point, you may recall the climax of *The Godfather*, where a series of brilliant executions is crosscut with the liturgy of a christening and irony is buried in the self-satisfaction of the double act.

That dramatic implication is lost in the technological wonder. In the summer of 1927, the many problems were dealt with:

the camera had to be soundproofed; the buzz in the Klieg lights was eliminated; the stage itself had to be a soundstage, devoid of extraneous noise; secret places were found for the microphones; and the camera and the disks were coordinated—by the time of the film's projection, there were fifteen reels of film and fifteen disks that had to be timed together. Not least, the performers had to learn to act and sing at the same time—Jolson had no greater asset than his understanding of that. But a moment came when he talked.

The plan was to have him sing several songs—at the beer hall, in his Broadway show, the Kol Nidre, but most important of all, with his mother, played by Eugenie Besserer with a doting, monotonous intensity. So Jolson sang and gave every song the thrust that was second nature to him. But then "it" happened, and apparently it was almost by chance.

Jack Robin, a star now, comes home to sing to his mother. The excellent research of Scott Eyman places the crucial moment as August 30.[13] Jack has just sung "Blue Skies" to his mother—it's a two shot, with Jack at the piano and Mama beside him. The singing is sugar—it's Irving Berlin, with Al doing a song he knew inside out. Then hesitation flowers. The son turns to his mother, and Jolson discovers an inner being. He speaks from the heart and mime is gone forever:

"Mama, darlin', if I'm a success in this show, well, we're gonna move from here. Oh yes, we're gonna move up in the Bronx. A lot of nice green grass up there and a whole lot of people you know. There's the Ginsbergs, the Guttembergs, and the Goldbergs. Oh, a whole lotta Bergs, I don't know 'em all.

"And I'm gonna buy you a nice black silk dress, Mama. You see Mrs. Friedman, the butcher's wife, she'll be jealous of you. . . . Yes, she will. You see if she isn't. And I'm gonna get you a nice pink dress that'll go with your brown eyes. . . ."

That repetition of G families could be composed and learned, but no script exists for it. As delivered, it sounds like

Jolson taking flight—it is his most jazzy improvisation—the words and the ideas spilling out, with "Yes, she will," which is unlikely as written but utterly natural as part of an actor's headlong glee.

Jack Warner said that Jolson did it all on the spur of the moment. When Sam heard it, he got writer Alfred Cohn to turn it into a written speech. Darryl Zanuck said it was *his* idea. He wondered, "Why doesn't Jolson turn to his mother and say . . ."[14] Sound engineer George Grovers said it was pure ad lib. Another onlooker believed it was a put up job between Sam and Jolson. And some said Jolson cried out, "No one will notice." The overall feeling at the studio was that it had been incidental, just one of those things.

If you look at the scene, over and over again, nothing saps the vitality of Jolson. It's as if he, and maybe he alone, understands exactly the new contact that is being opened up between performance and audience. Jack is talking to Mama, but Jolson is elated at the extra dimension. Here was a man who fed on live audience, and yet he has the instinct to sense a new flashpoint. And the theme is moving up in the world, being somebody (as the Warners gangster pictures would say), or—moving ahead fast—it's, "You told my story!," the final grasp of love that Clyde Barrow would have for Bonnie Parker in 1967.

Jackie and Jack are meant to be everyone's friend: he is sweet to his mother; he makes an ultimate sacrifice for his father; he admires Mary (May McAvoy), his costar in the Broadway show, just as he is an encouragement to everyone else involved. He would seem to be the receptacle of honest feeling, a good guy, a perfect mensch.

But Jolson in *The Jazz Singer* is a lot more complicated. He is so excited he is like a demon. And he is not a nice young man such as the story requires. By the most generous estimate he was forty-one when the film opened. Thus he was only six years younger than Warner Oland, the actor playing his father (and twelve years older than George Jessel). He looks and feels older —he is so far from the conventional juvenile who will make it in the show—the Dick Powell type at Warners in just a few years. He has a haunted face and a large head, with those demanding eyes and a huge brow. He has the intent gaze that could fit a villain, an evil mastermind, a mesmerist even. He could play Nosferatu, Dr. Mabuse, or the homegrown gangsters yet to come. This is not just his appearance, but the way he moves and his air of premeditation. He is coiled like a fighter, violent and so alive he seems hungry. At the rail depot, Jack sits on a tipped-up suitcase, writing a letter, where his stance is electric, elegant, and slightly dangerous. There is another strange moment when May McAvoy leaves him in close-up, and he dreams about her as if ready to devour her.

His sweetness is deeper than adorable. He has something frightening about him, or of such authority you feel his power to take charge. This is a hint towards Bogart, Cagney, Bette Davis, and even James Dean, with a kind of screen personality that depends on the stealth of breathing and a sigh of secret thoughts. It is an essential Warner Brothers character: the riveting protagonist who leaves us wary or afraid. Because the actor has taken over the moment, and then elected to pause. You see it in Cagney, Dean, and Bugs Bunny. Hesitation reminds us of power. This Jolson could be Dracula—in fact, Bela Lugosi opened on Broadway in that play one day before *The Jazz Singer* premiered. That is a coincidence, of course, but it is a telling concurrence in the history of performed personality and our willingness to embrace something decisive and sudden. (If you want another sign of immediacy in the times, Jack Dempsey versus Gene Tunney, the fight of the long count, had been just two weeks earlier in Chicago.)

The Jazz Singer changed everything, including the balance of power among the brothers. Sam is still hard to figure, but he had bet his life on sound and he had persevered with its mechanics. In doing so, he had opposed Harry and taught Jack that that policy could work. So Jack was liberated, and free to voice a sentimental verdict on his dead brother: "He was a man who was never selfish or vain, he would not even ask to be remembered. . . . The soaring shaft of sound film still stands, and brings to our lives laughter and tears and escape from daily stress. Sam brought it into the world, and gave his own life in exchange."

9

Now

BY THE EARLY 1930s, riding the waves, Warners had days when the brothers could feel they were in the lead. Unprecedented sums of new revenue were coming their way, and production responded. The audience was facing hard times, but that was gasoline for the confidence at Warners. No other studio did hard times with the same panache. Sound became irresistible in a matter of months, and it carried Warners to the top of the business. It was a national company all of a sudden, and a promise of fun.

But there was something awkward in the fun. The glory days of the talking picture are those of Depression and war, during which the Warner brothers (and every other Hollywood boss) became very rich and nearly royal figures, adept at persuading themselves that they were really for the people, the masses, the strangers—that mob of the disappointed and even the dangerous that alarms Nathanael West in *The Day of the Locust* (1939), when a movie première may turn into a riot.

In those days, the Hollywood system wanted to believe in its implicit contract with the public: buy a ticket and we'll cheer you up—you won't have to be afraid, for now. That uneasy deal made the films celebrated in this book. And Warners deserved the reputation for being ahead of its rivals. The brothers did read the papers; they saw what was coming in Europe; they wanted the American dream to be enlightened and responsible, so long as it didn't spoil their own dream of being resplendent and unquestioned moguls. The developing conflict between Harry and Jack was a matter of attitude. Harry was ready to let worry show. Jack insisted on his cocksure act. Harry had a sense of posterity, while Jack was all here and now, with a joke to close the show and settle doubts. So Warners owned the snappy answer.

Jack would say anything, for effect. The screenwriter Casey Robinson was fired once by Jack, over the phone—"I just want you to know, smart ass, that you will walk into a Warner Brothers studio again only over my dead body!"

He hung up. Robinson was gone. Then time passed, and Robinson was back on another project, and taken to see Jack. They had never met before. Robinson took a chance; he reminded Jack of the phone call. The comic in Jack grinned, "Well, I must be dead! How's your health? Welcome to Warner Brothers!"[1]

In silent pictures, characters had uttered, and then intertitles had delivered their speeches *as print*. It was like translation, slow and formal. But with sound, urgent crosstalk could occur *now*, like an itch being scratched. And because it was now, the spoken stuff didn't have to be Gettysburg addresses or fulsome love testaments. It could be, "You dirty rat!" or "I'd kiss you, but I've just washed my hair"—those impulsive remarks that can surprise the person saying them, as well as the listener. Things an actor might have thought of on the spur of a moment, as if to add, "Screw the writer, screw the Warner brothers. This is *me, now."* As if actors were people. But it was at Warner Brothers that actors and actresses were most aroused by saying stuff.

To pretend to history: a once-minor studio, rescued from its natural state of poverty by a willing dog, had become not just a force but the unwitting purveyor of insurrectionary sound and a production base that did gangster pictures and a new kind of showbiz musical like kids doing handstands.

It was also the one outfit where it seemed possible that some boss was asking out loud, "Look, is this 1931, 1932, or whatever? So what are we saying about *now?* And what are we doing to make movies matter?" If the country was in a crisis— and that idea was gaining ground—then shouldn't movies be there for the emergency? It was part of this mood that Warner films seemed to move, talk, and shoot quicker than others.

Darryl Zanuck often claimed to be that voice (and ready to shout down rivals), and in 1932 he wrote a letter to *The Hollywood Reporter* advocating what he called "a headline story": "It must not be confused with the gangster or underworld cycle of productions that have flooded the theatres in the past. Somewhere in its makeup it must have the punch and smash that would entitle it to a headline on the front page of any successful metropolitan daily."[2]

So much of silent cinema had been literary. It was drawn from plays, novels, the classical repertoire of history—the Bible, even! This was natural, but it could be pretentious, tiring, and archaic; it was an effort to convince society (and the filmmakers) that movies were serious and worthy, instead of *now.* Even *The Jazz Singer* had had an achingly old-fashioned moral purpose so much at odds with the immediacy of sound. The breakthrough picture had also been a retreat to an enclosing and fatuous past.

Talking pictures didn't have to be that way. In Europe, there were documentaries made just before sound that simply dwelled on what was happening as time passed. Films like *Berlin: Sym-*

phony of a Great City and *Man with a Movie Camera* were capti-
vated by an exciting new relationship between this recording
device (movie) and what was out there waiting to be seen and
heard. America had seldom enjoyed this relationship, but sound
insisted on it. In just a few years, from Berlin, Christopher Ish-
erwood would suggest, "I am a camera," foreseeing so many
new technologies and the bereft human condition that came
with them. But in the empire of silent cinema, the pious assumption had been, "We are a theatre." Still, a few people were
reckoning that if you stood on a street corner for ten minutes,
the untidy elements of a movie might appear. If you really understood the stupid, accepting nature of a camera.

At the end of *I Am a Fugitive from a Chain Gang* (1932), its
stricken hero, James Allen (Paul Muni), is reunited for a moment with his girl. He has found her just to say farewell. But he
cannot stay long, for fear of being recaptured. His life is root-
less and unlit, forever on the run; he is that American who must
always keep moving in one of the few films that understands
how tormented that urge can be.

"How do you live?" the girl asks him, as touched and troubled as any viewer of the film. We see Allen as the outline of a
face receding into darkness. "I steal," he says, savage and without self-pity, and then he reenters the night. It is one of the
great punch lines in American films, and eighty-five years later
it sustains the aching present tense in the title. For Allen is still
a fugitive in an America where fairness can be as remote or ab-
surd as ever. So we are left to ask ourselves, "What are escapist
movies for?," and few asked that question more pointedly than
this Vitaphone picture.

That conclusion was settled at the last minute, and it was
the decision of Darryl Zanuck (he said). Or was the ending a
beneficiary of chance: as they shot that last scene, did the lights
on the set really fail, so that the image disappeared? If that was
a mistake, in which Allen was consumed by darkness, director

Mervyn LeRoy and Zanuck would say they realized that the chance effect was better than their intentions. So they kept the error and it became classic. It's a lovely Warneresque story, but something very close to the effect was already in the script by Howard Green and Brown Holmes.[3]

Sometimes, in later years, when the Production Code had tried to soften the edge of 1932, that ending was dropped. But today it is judged to be the essential conclusion to Zanuck's most unremitting film, and one of the movies that most indicates Warner Brothers. The ending hurts more than the spectacular death throes of any of the studio's gangsters. James Allen is the most wounded Everyman figure out of Warner Brothers. *I Am a Fugitive* refuses to exclude the prospect that another kind of film—hopeless yet ecstatic—was possible.

The film is shockingly simple and direct; it never feels pondered over, and barely a moment seems composed for its own sake. This is the cinema of journalism. Allen returns from the war, decorated, older and wiser. His mother and his unctuous prelate brother want him to resume the old clerical job that has been kept open for him. But Allen learned engineering in the army. He wants to build and do new things. So he dodges the drab job lined up for him and branches out. But he gets nowhere and is not far from being a vagrant when he is involved in a minor holdup in a diner. He is sentenced to the chain gang. This is remorselessly unfair, but there is never a hint of legal maneuvers that might free him. (It's as if Allen is black now.) He goes away to do his time, like a leaf in the wind. And this plight is one that we feel in the square, naked face of Paul Muni.

This is the very year in which Muni overacted as Tony Camonte in *Scarface*. In *I Am a Fugitive*, he has the sense to trust the tragic story. We know Allen is a decent man, with worthy ambitions and ability; so the trap that closes on him is more desperate than the elegant fatalism in a Fritz Lang film. Seen today, Muni looks a lot like Ronald Reagan (no one knew that in 1932), which is enough to remind us now that Reagan-esque nice guys can turn out hopeless cases if they are not saved by acting, elections, and the celebrity status of those roles. We never feel starriness or self-confidence in Muni's Allen. He seems ordinary and unlucky, just as most movie leads are blessed and glamorous. The mainstream of American movies, then and now, has not liked to admit that bad luck can kill us.

The film's chain gang is a hellish place, a deliberate dwelling in the horrors of institutional life, and a warped but cruel concentrated camp. This involves the nightmare of the chains, the senselessness of breaking rocks and lives at the same time, the wretched food, the demeaning attitudes, and the lash. Though *I Am a Fugitive* does not exploit violence (as the gangster films did), its impact is harsh and terrifying. The lashing is conveyed in sound, more than in visuals, but the screams are unforgettable (and more wounding, I think, than the whipping in *12 Years a Slave*). This prison life is a mockery of every American ideal—except that American free expression has delivered it. So Allen makes a desperate escape, and tries to become the citizen he might have been.

He gets a construction job in which his talent is noticed. He is promoted; he becomes successful and prosperous; he marries—though the woman (Glenda Farrell) proves to be a heartless slut, and it is suggested that she informs on him. Thus fate closes in again and he is recaptured. Like an idiot—and this is the one touch of implausibility in the film—he falls for the offered deal (based on his new respectability) of going back to prison for ninety days in return for a pardon. That contract revels in torture, because we guess it's a trick. So Allen rediscovers his earlier hopelessness and is driven to a second escape, in which he blows up a bridge—thus mocking the straight life he yearned for. This second escape leaves him as the haunted fugitive at the end of the movie. In his life of darkness there are newspaper stories glimpsed that ask, "Is he too just another forgotten man?" (The picture was released in November 1932, a week after the election of Roosevelt, and just a few months before the opening of *Gold Diggers of 1933*, with its poignant song, "Remember My Forgotten Man.")

That sounds like an agenda, yet we don't know how organized Zanuck's thinking was—or how far it was put before Jack or Harry Warner for approval. Harry especially was high-minded, and eager to save the world, but he was deeply conservative and opposed to the ideas that chance could be fatal, or that rescue need be radical. But Zanuck did promote a leftist attitude at Warners, hiring writers who would prove to be leftists. One of these was John Bright, a full-fledged Communist, who helped write *The Public Enemy, Taxi!* and *Blonde Crazy*. He regarded Zanuck as "a tin pot Mussolini," yet he respected the producer's competence and authority.[4]

But in the spring of 1933, offended by studio orders for salary cuts across the board, Zanuck quit Warners and was on his way to Twentieth Century–Fox, where he would be known for his social conscience but was never again as tough. His celebrated *The Grapes of Wrath* for Fox (directed by John Ford) is a testament to that history, but its rather self-conscious poetry leaves the stark splendor and unhealed realism of *I Am a Fugitive* painfully clear.

Any trained Hollywood spectator watching the 1932 film expects relief, if not a happy ending. Next year's *Baby Face* does turn soft and ready for love at its close. But nothing comes to ease James Allen's closing darkness. The title stayed *I Am a Fugitive . . .* and surely hunched figures leaving the theatre in 1932 looked warily at their fellows, and at themselves.

As directed by Mervyn LeRoy, the film is made like a newspaper story: the filming is emphatic and cocksure, greedy for action and faces; and the editing hurtles forward, never diverted from the anguish in Muni's performance, but not milking it for pathos. Every record suggests that Zanuck controlled that editing. It's striking how swiftly the idioms of sound narrative had been adopted. The taut simplicity understands the finality of the script and its dark and unsentimental sense of America. It leaves our contemporary gangster films looking fancy and indulgent, and without a thought of changing the world.

In his memoir, Jack Warner was proud of what he called "our celluloid preachment against brutality" in *I Am a Fugitive*.[5] He even claimed that the movie "forecast the end of the chain gang system." But that penal format lasted in the South until 1955, and even now the *New York Times* is full of stories of corruption, brutality, and torture by guards at Rikers Island (on top of whatever prisoners have been doing to each other as a matter of course). The mark of shallow-minded reformism is its belief that it has succeeded. *I Am a Fugitive from a Chain Gang* is proof of there never being an excuse for complacency. In fact, the Robert E. Burns who wrote the book that prompted the film, and who had led a life like that of James Allen, was arrested late in 1932, still on the run. (He had secretly advised Warners on details of the film.) He might have been deported to Georgia to serve more time, and he was reckless in helping promote the film (he seems to have felt he was a celebrity), but the governor of New Jersey refused to sign the deportation order. Still, it was 1945 before Burns was officially pardoned by the state of Georgia.

I Am a Fugitive reminds us of people still lost in this great nation. The journalistic style has a punch that hurts today. It's far more corrosive than the celebrated *Baby Face*, the last Warner Brothers film on which Zanuck had one of his names—he was the Mark Canfield who gets credit for the original story behind a script written by Gene Markey and Kathryn Scola. (Zanuck was paid $1 for the story.) *Baby Face* is fascinating still; and it was startling enough in 1933 to be censored. Nevertheless, it's a film that loses its nerve in a traditional Hollywood way that is boastful yet compromised.

It opens in Erie, Pennsylvania, in a speakeasy overlooking industrial smokestacks. Lily's father owns the joint, and uses her as sexual bait to attract customers. At twenty-six, in a cotton dress and a flimsy top, Lily (Barbara Stanwyck) passes as a common tart. But why does she linger in this pit at Stanwyck's age and with the star's cynical aplomb? The actress was willing to help the picture and aware that she was playing a kind of hooker. She suggested that Lily do a dance—close to nude—for the speakeasy customers, but the studio rejected that.

One of the customers, a gloomy, older man, Cragg (Alphonse Ethier), out of Eugene O'Neill, offers Lily Nietzsche's *Will to Power* to read and wonders, "Why don't you get out?" That is the call of so many American films to the young and ambitious. It is what haunts James Allen; and as escapism or the dream of self-invention, it is an idea embedded in Hollywood's decades-long advertisement for itself—be *unum*, not *e pluribus*. Cragg tells Lily she could possess power (it turns out later that her name is Lily Powers). "You must be a master, not a slave," he says. "All life is exploitation." (This view of America had to be trimmed in New York state to get the film licensed.)

He says a woman has no chance—and truly she is being given advice generally kept for men—but Cragg tells her women have power that they must use. Lily gets the message—which means that Stanwyck glows with a wan, sardonic smile as if to say, all right then. Some enthusiasts feel this is Stanwyck at her best, but her role is cursorily written, and lacking in the warmth and humor—the spirit—that so often distinguished this actress. She is allowed to be street-smart, sly, and cynical, but at the expense of real intelligence. Lily's conversion is not felt; it's just a convenient trigger for what follows.

The father is killed when his still explodes, and only then

does Lily leave Erie (with her friend, a black maid, played by Theresa Harris). They ride the rails, and when a railroad guard orders them off the train, Lily cocks an eye at the maid to get lost while she persuades the guard. (Why can't the maid get some, too—or is she just decoration?) This is the start of Lily's rise to mastery. In the city, she takes on the Gotham Trust Company, gets a job by sleeping with an obese assistant in Personnel, and then seduces higher bosses, like rungs on a ladder, until one of these men kills a rival and then shoots himself.

Some commentary still exults in this alleged reversal of the usual order, and its exposé of how feeble and dishonest men can be. But you only have to look at Louise Brooks's Lulu in *Pandora's Box* (made in Germany in 1929) to appreciate the grim inroads on real adventuresses. Lulu is more candid sexually than Lily is allowed to be—more naked, more needy, more triumphant and fatalistic. She's more committed to her adventure. But her conquests are leading to death, so it is a sweet convenience that Lily never gets pregnant, diseased, beaten, or anywhere near the knife that waits for Lulu in the hands of Jack the Ripper. *Baby Face* is a cute display case for the "daring" eroticism of Lily and Stanwyck, but as inherently chaste as all American movies, even those made before the Code.

Baby Face falters as a work when Lily confronts the board of the bank—the Bank, if you prefer—as the scarlet woman who has caused a scandal and who is looking for a payoff. This is when we feel Lily's unreality, or vacancy. As she has risen, she has had her hair done and bought better clothes. Some of her men are iconically acceptable—they include Donald Cook and a young John Wayne. But the film never bothers with pleasure or romantic interest. In 1933, some audiences felt they were shocked, as well as amused, though the depiction of Lily is more limited than the film's alleged daring suggests. The camera roams her legs a few times, and there is some innuendo, but it's coy and calculated. A regular viewer, trained in how movies functioned, could reasonably predict—in 1933, or now—that the hardboiled Lily needs to fall in love to be saved.

That begins at the bank board meeting to discuss the scandal. The new president is a recent playboy, Courtland Trenholm (George Brent), and he is alert to Lily's claim for $15,000 to keep her from divulging her diary to the newspapers. Instead, he takes her up on the plea that she wants a serious job and sends her off to the Paris office to get her away from attention (an awkward, ill-written scene that defeats director Alfred E. Green). But for the first time, her pout has to concede that a man has handled her. How much more challenging the film would be if it let Lily realize that she might take over the Bank itself.

Never mind, for the man is in love, that mood in which one movie star must lean towards another. Courtland may have been a roué, but he is a "nice," man, thoughtful and discerning. Quite soon, he visits Paris himself. The couple spend days and nights together. He is infatuated enough to give her bonds, cash, and jewels to fill a pigskin case. In truth, he regards her as a "Baby Face," but then she sighs and says, "I'd love to have a 'Mrs.' on my tombstone." (One hopes Zanuck didn't write that inglorious line.)

Then (in the way of the early thirties) the Bank fails and Courtland is indicted for responsibility. The movie assures us that he was *not* responsible—who was, in the early thirties?—but he needs the contents of that pigskin case for a bail bond. At first Lily is reluctant: "I can't do it. I have to think of myself. All the gentleness and kindness have been destroyed." She plans to return to France with her proceeds, but just before the boat leaves, her heart softens. She hurries back to Courtland's building to find that he has attempted suicide. So there's a rush to the hospital and the clear suggestion that her pigskin funds are going to be needed. She breaks down in tearful admissions: "Oh darling, don't leave me. I'll do anything for you. I love you so much." Though weak, he smiles at her in the ambulance and begins to be healed. The world is going to be all right for Mr. and Mrs. Courtland Trenholm. Nietzsche might turn in his grave.

But why shouldn't the ex-playboy prove an inept disaster at the Bank, and why shouldn't Lily watch his disgrace with her bitter but intelligent smile? That could be as scathing and radical as *I Am a Fugitive*, especially if Lily set the bank straight. But the condition of filmgoing in those days was not really prepared to face the ways in which Lily thrives on self-sufficient sexual gratification—as well as pigskins of plunder. And surely our society was as reluctant to face such things as it was to admit that the Depression had been predictable, manipulated, a source of ruinous suffering for many and great benefit for a few.

Baby Face is an opportunistic and condescending title. It's a way of nudging us and saying, watch out, that pretty girl could be sleeping her way to the top and not noticing that she had a chance to be as smart and demanding as Bette Davis's later roles at Warner Brothers, and as much a rival to male assurance. Everybody loves Stanwyck (we say) because she had wit, sexiness, warmth, and compassion; men desired her as much as women wanted to be like her. But in a few films—like *Double Indemnity* and *The File on Thelma Jordon*—she was capable of delivering cold, ruthless intelligence. Alas, to get there, she had to be insane—and destroyed by those films. What 1933 needed— as much as we need it today—were films that saw that a woman might be not just a Powers but a power, if only because men who look at women as if they exist on a screen are such idiots that you may have to teach them how to commit suicide when disgrace comes along.

So *Baby Face* is amusing and naughty in a naïve, self-protective way, and it's reasonable to invoke it as the sort of film that bumped against the nervousness of the Production Code. But its saddest defect is imposing the caution of the Code on itself, before it might have been compelled to do so.[6] One lesson in this, then and now, is that it has been easier for movies to celebrate smart, ruthless and attractive figures if they are men. The dolls, the dames, the baby faces, could be sexy, bold, and wisecracking until it was time to tell their men, "I'll do anything for you."

That sappy tone would be changed only by the manly ego named Bette Davis.

Joan Blondell—singer, dancer, sweetheart, loyalist

10

My Forgotten Man

THERE WAS NO immediate move to call *The Jazz Singer* a "musical," though it was, plainly, a melodrama with heard music and singing, as well as a movie in which this new element—musical accompaniment—existed without labor or friction. *The Jazz Singer* could as easily be regarded as a version of the Faust legend for Jews in show business—but it carried way beyond that hard core to what we call the general public. And why would an American movie cater only to Jews? Wasn't Hollywood a place where certain Jewish impresarios strove to become American? But the definition of the film's genre was confused by the overwhelming Al Jolson.

So Warner Brothers did the natural thing, and as quickly as it could. It offered the same again. For Vitaphone once more, Warners cast Jolson as Al Stone in *The Singing Fool*. It's still not exactly what we'd call a musical today, according to the 1950s heyday of the genre. Rather, it's a sob story with songs, and a warning to reckless male ambition. But the songs arise naturally because it's another story about a singer. When the picture opens, Al Stone is a waiter in a nightclub. He looks like a waiter, granted that he has Jolson's consuming head and eyes—and granted that the film introduces him with a coy "surprise" close-up where a table is lowered on the floor revealing Al, well aware that we're waiting for him, in love with him. The role seems humble, but not the actor. It is his picture, and after *The Jazz Singer* Jolson demanded $150,000 for the job, to be paid in Warners stock.

But he does look forty-eight, which is mature for a waiter hoping for his breakthrough as a singer. Stone is loved by Grace (Betty Bronson), a brunette cigarette girl at the restaurant, but like a chump he prefers the chill blonde beauty of Molly (Josephine Dunn), a speakeasy singer. Of course, as the film gets under way, Stone finds his chance—he sings "It All Depends on You" (he means Molly) and "There's a Rainbow Round My Shoulder," and soon he's "Sittin' on Top of the World." As a star, he marries Molly. They have a son. Then a few years pass and Al is older, more gaunt, and a good deal less likely. In all the frenzy over Al Jolson, we have to admit how unsuited to romantic glory he was. Seen in close-up, Jolson didn't match the small, exuberant figure dominating a stage. They were different guys.

The Singing Fool is closer to a talking picture than *The Jazz Singer*, and it was made in exultation as sound began to transform the business, which meant that other studios had to buy into Warners' expertise. Apart from its songs, there are extended dialogue scenes: notably a chat between Al and his infant son (Davey Lee). But there are still silent scenes with intertitles. It's directed by Lloyd Bacon, for the most part with a placid camera and long takes—though the film opens with a display of camera movement that serves no purpose beyond misleading the audience. The story is dire. Molly grows bored with Al;

she dumps him and leaves with Sonny Boy. Al goes into free fall, not just loss of career and depression, but not shaving, and aging fast. He looks over fifty, and rather frightening. There's one scene of him on the street, shabby in a heavy fedora that shadows his face, that could be from *I Am a Fugitive from a Chain Gang*.

Of course, things pick up, though the sick son dies—Al sings "Sonny"—but the fallen Stone regains his luster and marries the patient if foolish Grace. Things are going to be all right, which seems a pity eighty years later because one can feel a tragic actor lurking in Jolson. He was too old and strange for sunny parts. His singing voice verged on hysteria. He was ready for some operatic venture—he might have carried off the lyric anger and ruined romantic in Sondheim's *Sweeney Todd*.

The Singing Fool, though not much seen today, can be said to have been more important than *The Jazz Singer*, which was actually hard to see because so few theatres had the technology for it. A year later, with sound systems spreading, *The Singing Fool* drew huge audiences eager to catch up—and Jolson uses his catchphrase, "You ain't heard nothing yet," several times.[1] On a budget of less than $400,000, the film grossed more than $5 million, a million more than *The Jazz Singer*.

Two days after *The Singing Fool* opened, on September 21, 1928, Jolson married Ruby Keeler. She was still only eighteen, from Nova Scotia, though she had been a spectacular tap dancer at Tex Guinan's clubs since her early teens. He was forty-two (he said; others said plus four), married and divorced twice already. Jolson saw Keeler playing on stage in *Show Girl* and—apparently—joined in with her, singing from his seat (who needed scriptwriters?). The audience was dazzled, and Al was co-opted into the show. No, I don't believe it, either.

As innocent as this showbiz life could leave her, Ruby was overwhelmed by the huge star and his burning eyes. When Jack Warner approached Jolson—about putting Ruby in *42nd*

Street—Jolson assumed *he* was being offered a part; when he realized it was Ruby Warner was after, Al required a $10,000 finder's fee. He didn't want to play with her (because of looking too old), but he hated watching her kissing other guys—like Dick Powell. So he fretted and acted as her manager. It sounds like a marriage (it ended in 1940) that deserves its own film—if only someone had had the wit and nerve to let the two stars play themselves. Instead, they were put in films where that real life was coyly alluded to (but evaded).

As an inescapable father figure to the Warners musical, Jolson was overbearing, interfering, and, finally, outdated. He would linger at the studio until the mid-thirties, but he was notably absent from what are now thought of as the great Warners musicals of 1932–33. Maybe he seemed too tied to the sentimental celebration of Jewish tradition. Only a few years after *The Jazz Singer* and *The Singing Fool*, the studio wanted to make clear that it was "young and healthy" and available to everyone. The underground story by which Hollywood Jews separated themselves from their own cultural tradition is as complex and revealing as the way Warners would discover the chance of making a fortune on stories about people who held up banks. The studio had mixed feelings about Jolson. In 1946, when *The Jolson Story* was set up, with Al singing the songs (at sixty) and doing "Swanee" in long shot, Warners let the project be done at Columbia. Larry Parks played Jolson, and Evelyn Keyes was his wife, though Ruby Keeler refused to let her name be used in the film.[2]

The musical was floundering in the early 1930s. It hadn't really been opened up yet in that there were no films in which song and dance carried a plot. Harry Warner let it be known that he couldn't give them away. But then, according to the man himself, Darryl Zanuck persevered and saw the chance of a new kind of musical, as typified by *42nd Street*. Its novelty lay in what we call the "back-stage" narrative format. Maybe the public loved song and dance sequences. In just a few years they went to see Fred Astaire and Ginger Rogers for those "numbers," and they were indifferent to the alleged storylines that set them up. But there was a terror of literal-mindedness in those who made musicals: how would people feel comfortable with the bizarre and irrational way that characters suddenly broke into song? This dilemma is at the heart of those breakthrough musicals from 1933.

So, if you care to believe this, Zanuck thought he would try a musical, without letting either Harry or Jack Warner realize what he was doing.[3] This is fanciful enough to come from another musical. There was a novel, by Bradford Ropes, who had been a dancer, and Zanuck bought the screen rights: it was the story of a group of people trying to mount a musical in the worst days of the Depression. There was an impresario, Julian Marsh, who was going frantic and risking his own health by doing this. There was a self-important woman star in the show, and there were the brash American kids. At the last minute the stuffy star, Dorothy Brock, breaks an ankle and wow! The kid understudy, Peggy Sawyer, goes on and she is a sensation. Which is very tidy because she's falling in love with the cheeky male lead, Billy Lawler. Have you heard this story before?

Early thoughts of Richard Barthelmess and Warren William were set aside, and Warner Baxter was cast as Julian. He's rather good; he seems to feel he's playing a character and is required to act, and he never sings; it happens that he looks like a hefty Darryl Zanuck. Bebe Daniels was Dorothy, Ruby Keeler was Peggy, and Dick Powell was Billy.

Powell was a kid from Mountain View, Arkansas, who had gone from the church choir to making records, and from there to a contract with Warners when they bought out his recording label, Vocalion. He was nice looking; he had a pleasant light voice—though he disliked singing. He could carry a line, and he was in his twenties, with a grin that suggested a naughty mind.

He matched Zanuck's instinct that movie musicals were for kids who had never seen a stage show. On screen, Dick Powell was the spirit of the Warners musical—once you overlooked the girls. But Dick had that sly, know-all manner that said to the audience, "Do you realize I'm up here with all these half-dressed girls—which is like half-undressed—and you're not? No wonder I'm grinning!" That grin was vital at Warner Brothers, and it was the human behavior in which Jack Warner himself was closest to the enterprise.

Then there were the gifted songwriters, Harry Warren and Al Dubin. Together, they wrote "Forty-Second Street," "You're Getting to Be a Habit with Me," "Shuffle Off to Buffalo," and "Young and Healthy." Chances are you can recall those songs as I list them, and if you go back to see the movie, the tunes will last in your head for days. They're not great or heartfelt songs, but they're cute and winning. For the most part the Warner Brothers musical ducked sincerity or intensity—the very qualities that had made *The Jazz Singer* old-fashioned. But you can believe that the mischievous Powell has just thought of them and they are songs that move—the Warners musical never rested; scenes slid into other scenes before boredom had a chance to gather; and motion on screen was always as important as the chance of emotion.

But none of these elements would have meant much without the "gaze" of the films, and there we have the genius of Busby Berkeley, who was officially the choreographer on dance sequences, but who gradually took over whole films and supplanted official directors, like Lloyd Bacon or Mervyn LeRoy. William Berkeley Enos was born in Los Angeles in 1895, and he was one of the greatest talents Warners had.[4] He was a demon, and not always a nice guy. He went through wives the way his camera tracked through the legs of chorus girls. He was the driver in an automobile smash-up in 1935 that killed a couple of people, and he was acquitted after two hung juries. Even the good-natured Joan Blondell admitted that he was like a general with his army. Almost before anyone noticed, "Buzz" had these vast sets with a camera high aloft, and masses of girls, pianos, and . . . waterfalls. Blondell told a story about the shoot for the "By a Waterfall" number in *Footlight Parade*, when a couple of girls went into the water and were never found again.[5] She was kidding, of course, and these musicals kidded everything. But there was not a director in Hollywood who had such rigorous control of what was happening—and Berkeley was not even credited as a director yet. The system appreciated his technology before grasping its meaning. In addition, he never asked auditioning girls to dance—he just looked at them and kept the prettiest girls up front in the ensembles.

By 1935, in the range of cinema there were two directors, or auteurs, who had presided over the choreography of human groups with similar vision and ruthless authority—I am thinking of Sergei Eisenstein in the Soviet Union and Leni Riefenstahl with *Triumph of the Will*. Am I saying Berkeley was totalitarian or fascist? He was a creator on film, and just as Riefenstahl idealized the uniformed male figure, so Busby Berkeley was mad for the female losing her clothes. Which do we prefer? People still smile at the geometric formations Buzz organized, the girls in the pool opening and closing their legs, fellating the water, blooming Os. It's as if the erotic extravaganza is still too much, or too daring to be talked about. But this is the orgy of pre-Code cinema far more than the suggestiveness in a film like *Baby Face*. In the "Honeymoon Hotel" number from *Footlight Parade*, the sense of imminent abandon is not just lubriciously present—it is flagrant, mocking of propriety, and blithely filthy. This glorification of the American girl is entrancing and delirious but alarming. The girls are slaves; the camera is our vizier. In the figure of the lewd homunculus ogling it all—played by the nine-year-old Billy Barty—we are at a point where harem slapstick is becoming a portent of pornography. You realize how close the entertainment movie was to scrapping the orderly dreams America's happiness project was discussing. In just a few years, the pious sentimentality of Jolson's inauguration had become a pleasure dome of sexual ferment.

The conflict was giddy, and Hollywood realized that a Production Code was in the offing. That would impose many dumb restrictions (and stimulate prurient imaginations), but the factory was telling itself to be careful. Looking at *Convention City*, Jack Warner wrote to Hal Wallis: "We must put brassieres on Joan Blondell and make her cover up her breasts, otherwise we're going to have these pictures stopped in a lot of places. I believe in showing their forms but, for Lord's sake, don't let those bulbs stick out."[6] A year later, *Convention City* was banned and prints were destroyed. It is now said to be lost. Blondell admitted it was "the raunchiest thing there has ever been."[7]

Audiences born sixty years after 1933 "know" these numbers or their mood. They are emblems of the early thirties, of Warner Brothers, and the "innocent fun" of that era. We have glimpsed them on Turner Classic Movies, or streaming somewhere, and Berkeley had an instinct about what streaming meant long before that technology came into being. The daring of these films is more liberated (and disconcerting) than the violence in the gangster films. Cagney is the lead character in *Footlight Parade*, a punchy guy searching for a way of making promotional "prologues" for the new medium. That is the excuse for enormous set-piece numbers, including "By a Waterfall," which required a glass-sided pool, twenty feet by forty feet, and twenty thousand gallons of water a minute—all in flagrant defiance of hard times.

There is one sequence from these films that surpasses all others. It appears suddenly in *Gold Diggers of 1933*, and you realize that this searing depth might have been there all along. We seem to be watching a show on stage: the curtain goes up on a bare street set; a hobo picks up a discarded cigarette end, but before he can smoke it a woman appears—she is a prostitute, in a low-cut clingy blouse and no bra, she is Joan Blondell; she lights a full cigarette from the end and gives it to the guy. Then she leans against a lamp post and recites the words to the Warren/Dubin song "Remember My Forgotten Man." It is as if the sentiments expressed are too much for singing alone. The woman gets a rich close-up in the process and we attend to the words—about how a man who loved her was sent away.

There is a transition. The camera tilts up and to the side and we find another woman in a window who starts to sing the song—she is Etta Moten, black, and not credited on the film. The song carries on and is shown over windows of a Dorothea Lange–like nursing mother, and then an older woman who may have lost a son or a husband.

There is another transition, and the song becomes rousing now, like a march, as soldiers make a parade before going off to war with streamers in the air and a rejoicing crowd. But then the soldiers are on their own, at night, marching to some combat front in a forbidding rain.

And then this valiant column becomes a tattered troop after battle, wounded, bloodied, limping, diminished, demoralized, and that much older. The whole sequence is a pageant for regret, and a kind of betrayal. It will come back to Blondell again, singing her heart out and explaining why she has become a streetwalker:

> And once he used to love me
> I was happy then
> He used to take care of me
> Won't you bring him back again?
> 'Cause ever since the world began
> A woman's got to have a man
> Forgetting him, you see
> Means you're forgetting me

Like my forgotten man.

Audiences today may wince at "A woman's got to have a man," for Warners in 1933 was a chauvinist operation. But in 2017, how many American movies address underprivilege with this blazing eloquence?

Gold Diggers of 1933 is credited to Mervyn LeRoy, but I'm sure this scene was envisaged and done by Busby Berkeley. It is among the best ever made at Warner Brothers. When Zanuck and Jack Warner saw the sequence—in the early spring of 1933, just before Zanuck quit Warners—they agreed that it was the proper climax to the film and they moved it to the end of the picture. The ease with which the apparent stage show slips over into the panorama of the Great War is breathtaking, and it points to a kind of ambition over which the musical has always been very nervous. As well as a musical achievement, this is a six-minute epic of political statement. If you intercut it with some of the glorifying parades from *Triumph of the Will*, you would have a pageant of the 1930s, as well as a forecast of what was to come. You have to admit, whether it was intended or understood at the time, there was a spirit at Warners ready to confront such things, a spirit that leaves so much of Hollywood looking frivolous and escapist. That remembering woman could be on an American stamp. Seen today, she reminds us how far memory, or history, may be a lost cause.

Gold Diggers of 1933 was a triumph ($2.2 million revenue on a budget of $433,000). It inaugurated a run of Gold Digger films. That world was in a terrible crisis: the banks shut down and Hitler came to power in the same year. And here was a movie made in Burbank by many hands, but a marker in our history, aware that sometimes the whole of life could be expressed in a few moments from one routine picture.

11

Be Somebody

WHERE DOES IT BEGIN, this American passion for outlaw iden-
tification, as if bursting to admit that the land of the free and
the home of the brave may be a casino where nerve will finesse
virtue? Perhaps it's in the first lie told by a newcomer on the
bright shore—the disowning of any prior, humiliating, or con-
fining existence? Begin again in the new world? In the advertised land of equality there is still an underground motto of
never giving a sucker an even break. You can have Thomas Jef-
ferson, and Martin Luther King, but you have to take W. C.
Fields, too. And Donald Trump. We are close to the panache of
old Hollywood, and no studio wore it with more bravado than
Warners.

You find it everywhere, like speakeasies and the merry contempt for archaic morality. In 1925, on 42nd Street, Nick Car-
raway meets Jay Gatsby for lunch, but there is someone else
with them, "a small flat-nosed Jew" named Meyer Wolfsheim.

Mr. Wolfsheim knew Gatsby when he was Jimmy Gatz. "I made the pleasure of his acquaintance just after the war," Wolfsheim tells Nick. "But I knew I had discovered a man of fine breeding after I talked with him an hour. I said to myself, 'There's the kind of man you'd like to take home and introduce to your mother and sister.'"

Wolfsheim is grave and respectful over breeding and the scheme of mothers and sisters. He treasures Gatsby as "an Oggsford man." But Nick can't place this unexpected companion. "Who is he anyhow, an actor?" he asks Gatsby after Wolfsheim has moved on.

Gatsby says, no, he's a gambler, the man who fixed the World Series in 1919. Nick has heard of this—we all have—but he is amazed to think that one unimpressive man "could start to play with the faith of fifty million people—with the single-mindedness of a burglar blowing a safe."[1] Wasn't that a magic normally reserved for movie moguls?

"Why isn't he in jail?" Nick wonders, and Gatsby's reply has the bounce and shame that Fitzgerald could always handle. "They can't get him, old sport. He's a smart man."

Why aren't more of them in jail, now that it's more than fifty million whose faith is being played with, and when the versions of available gambling have become so much more sophisticated or genetic? It was some time in the late 1920s and the 1930s that America began to appreciate a new smartness that could collect cool millions and get out of jail free. You can feel this in the cultural rise of the gangster, but the shift doesn't just apply to outlaws. The secret of this transaction is how college men and women, well-born, well-educated, good-looking Americans, began to behave like sharks and frauds. And that has to do with the movies and Warner Brothers, the factory that almost copyrighted attractive gangsters. It's only when you put it that way and then look back at pictures of Jack Warner himself that you realize that he was trying to act like a rogue—

or like your favorite uncle pretending to be a suave Wolfsheim. Jack was in charge of it all, that was his talent or credential, and he had an instinct for covering up his real emptiness by seeming like a charming pirate.

Sound was the fuel for this creative gamble. It would be a long time before people in movies talked as well as Gatsby and Nick—you may decide that that has never really happened—but the insouciance in how they speak, the irony, and the feeling we have of things being left unsaid, those qualities are valued in movies after 1927. Moreover, *The Great Gatsby* has other sound cues: it has a moment where the brakes on a racing automobile squeal. But that "death car" didn't stop. And there is gunfire later on—"The chauffeur heard the shots." All we need to wrap those sound effects is the great swirl of music—let it be by Max Steiner—as if to underline the Warneresque wryness that lurks in that title, *The Great Gatsby*.

So even the stars may need to be retrieved from their own pool. The gangster film is subversive: it makes fun of prohibition—as if we had once reckoned to be moral, saved conservatives, instead of opportunists, addicts, headlong futurists and gamblers. We drank because the dream was failing, or we had failed it. It is the oiled celebrity of hoodlums and killers that flourished in those "dry" years. And it was the grease of sound being applied to the staid fables of silent cinema.

In addition, in 1929, the casino failed. For a moment that seemed merely a Wall Street melodrama, with tycoons and other climbers jumping out of their windows as stock prices plummeted. But soon the calamity came down on the nation and the dark fields of the republic like a curse. By the time of the first official gangster pictures, by 1930 onwards, America was suffering, and the box office with it. Between 1930 and 1932, U.S. unemployment rose from 8.7 to 23.6 percent. In the same period, movie attendance plunged by more than a third. But in Warners' *Gold Diggers of 1933*, Ginger Rogers sang the opening number, "We're in the Money," without dismay, in a costume made of coins.

We could assure ourselves that "the gangster" was a hoodlum who had to end up shot to pieces to satisfy decorum, but look at the fun and glory he'd have on the way. And Warners was more honest about hard times than any other studio. It was the factory system that defied the slump, and said, "The hell with the Depression!" American movies have seldom countenanced dismay (which doesn't eliminate it in life). As the box office faltered, Warners gave us dames, gunfire, jazzy music, wisecracks, and outrageous, unhindered ids in smart suits, guys who'll go for broke because they know they're doomed. It's an early version of *Breaking Bad*.

Here is Rico, at the start of *Little Caesar*, telling his friend Joe how it's going to be—and just wonder how far this could be a Jack Warner talking to himself as he practiced his take-a-meeting grin: "Yeah, money's all right, but it ain't everything. Yeah, be somebody. Look hard at a bunch of guys and know that they'll do anything you'll tell 'em. Have your own way or nothin'. Be somebody."[2]

In gangster pictures dandy outlaws confronted audiences who guarded their one frayed suit. Hollywood enjoyed that insolence and so in the early thirties, without shame or modesty, it made pictures with beautiful clothes and lustrous décor, with hoodlums rising in society. Pictures were a cash business, where somebody counted the take, reported one number and put another in his pocket. And part of the cash business was that it rubbed shoulders and wads with people who had unreported money they were ready to invest, without too many questions being asked. No one enjoyed gangster pictures more than gangsters; and few people did a better gangster routine than the men in charge.

A young man named Milton Sperling got a job as Darryl Zanuck's secretary at Warners. His first day on the job, he enters Zanuck's office to find Zanuck, Hal Wallis, James Cagney, and a few guys who must be writers.

> Suddenly, Darryl Zanuck popped up from behind his desk, aimed a polo mallet at me, and went on, "Rat-tat-tat-tat-tat-tat . . . " like the stick was a Tommy-gun. I stood there bewildered.
> "Fall down, you son-of-a-bitch, you're dead!" Zanuck screamed.
> He started shooting at me again with the polo stick, annoyed that his first bullet hadn't hit me and even more annoyed that I wouldn't fall down dead. I figured that he was acting out the way he wanted Cagney to assassinate his rival in a movie, so I dropped in a heap to the floor.[3]

That all turned out fine: the picture being formulated was *The Public Enemy*, which grossed around ten times what it cost, and in just a few years Sperling would marry Harry Warner's daughter Betty. Such magic happened, despite the flourish of boasting. One day Jack Warner met Albert Einstein—the new celebrity culture—and told the great man he had his own theory of relativity. "What's that?" asked Albert, eager to play straight man. "Never hire relatives," said Jack—but his type never heeded their own advice.[4]

Several people deserve credit for the Warner Bros gangster film, and many claimed the credit: the list starts with Darryl Zanuck, just because he was master of the lists (and kept a polo mallet in his office), but it includes a couple of directors, a few distinctively fresh movie stars, a gang of writers—and Jack himself. But the impulse of sound technology and the imperiled position of moviegoing as a business in the early thirties were just as important. It was as if the nation wasn't sure that gangsters might not have the answer on how to make the system work. The movies had stumbled into a new way of shooting people, with flame flowering from the muzzles of guns, the rat-tat-tat jazz beat and the screams. We still have that urban symphony in our heads; we are still uncertain about the gangster answer. In 2016 we had a presidential candidate who did a gangster act all year long.

W. R. Burnett was determined to write. He quit the calm of Columbus, Ohio, to be in Chicago itself; he took a job as night clerk in a cheap hotel, the Northmere; he had time to write there, and he had lowlifes to observe. Burnett was "appalled" by the big city and its human indifference. But he met gangsters and understood their feeling that life was a war with them as soldiers. His novel *Little Caesar* was published soon after the St. Valentine's Day Massacre of 1929, and its protagonist, Rico, was "a composite figure that would indicate how men could rise to prominence or money under the most hazardous conditions."[5] Burnett had Al Capone as a model, but he also thought of Macbeth, and he gave his book a motto from Machiavelli: "The first law of every being is to preserve itself and live. You sow hemlock, and expect to see ears of corn ripen."

No one on the film bothered to notice, but that was politics, with as much relevance to fascist Europe as to the possible new deal and FDR. Warners has long had a reputation for liberalism, and that theory is tenable if you're an automatic optimist. But a ruthless practicality was there, too, and that has only one ideal—have someone in charge.

Burnett's book was hailed as the first gangster novel, and it impressed everyone at Warners. They were encouraged by the success of von Sternberg's *Underworld* (1927) at Paramount. There were several scripts passed around, before Francis Edwards Faragoh did a persuasive rewrite taken from Rico's sardonic point of view. The script was given to Mervyn LeRoy, never highly regarded by those who believed in great directors, but a crucial figure at Warners (and in 1934, having divorced one wife, LeRoy would marry another of Harry Warner's daughters, Doris). But when you watch *Little Caesar*, you don't notice direction or authorial vision. You see and hear Edward G. Robinson.[6]

Emanuel Goldenberg had been born in Bucharest in 1893, and he came to America at the age of ten with a family that had been harassed by antisemitism. He thought he would be a lawyer—he was a serious and responsible young man, who would acquire left-wing ideals that eventually got him into trouble—but he turned to acting and changed his name to Robinson. He worked in New York with the Yiddish theatre, and his natural talents emerged. He was short, with a big personality. He had a rather squashed, ugly face, a low, growling voice, yet he was as alert as a young lover. In fact, Robinson hardly ever got to play romantic roles, but in 1927 he had a huge success on Broadway as a vicious gangster, Nick Scarsi, in a play called *The Racket*, by Bartlett Cormack—just imagine Robinson snarling "Nick Scarsi." The movies heard this, and the uncommonly gentle, humane side to Robinson began to be erased.

Burnett was happy to have *Little Caesar* made (it changed his life), but he thought Warners made it more conventional. That didn't matter. "What made the picture was Robinson," said the novelist.[7] He snarled and he sighed with self-rapture—"I'm Caesar Fredrico Bandello," he says, the syllables falling like blood or wine. He is self-obsessed: his clothes, his authority, the stories about him in the press—he and the whole movie are wild about newspapers. He disdains women, he kills rivals, and he knows as well as we do where he's going. That guaranteed destination is a license for mayhem, leading to the heartfelt, "Mother of mercy—is this the end of Rico?" He dies without regret, full of wonder that his flame could be snuffed out, trying to comb his hair. It's still one of the great lines, repeated in our playacting; it's the snarl as aria—Ben Hecht called it a "cello staccato."[8]

Rico has to die. But Robinson and gangster pictures were made. *Little Caesar* opened January 9, 1931, at seventy-nine minutes. Warners had to run it twenty-four hours a day with mounted police controlling the lines. Everyone said it was a smash hit, though no one actually owned up to how much money it made. You didn't follow the money in those days, not if you wanted to keep some of it.

The bounty can be read in what happened. By the mid-thirties there had been more than three hundred gangster pictures, or movies sold under that sign. Not all of them came from Warners, but that studio had the knack and the reputation. It was the hard-boiled factory, and some inmates added that it was run like a prison. You can attribute that to Zanuck, LeRoy, and a few writers, yet the public knew that the deal was with the actors—Robinson, George Raft eventually, and even Bogart later. But at the heart of it all was Jimmy Cagney. Between 1930 and 1939, he made thirty pictures for Warners, and most of them with Jimmy as a hood or a good guy who acted like a hood. His fellow actor Pat O'Brien (they did eight pictures together—Cagney did eleven with Frank McHugh) said he was as much of that era as Babe Ruth, Jack Dempsey, and speakeasy hostesses. He was Irish—he was a gentle, quiet guy in life and a family man—but he photographed like a featherweight devil, full of violent urges and sniping back talk. He was dangerous on screen; it was what he had instead of sex. He might kill anyone, devour an actress, or turn into a dancing machine. No one had ever moved like Cagney, or seemed such a feral, animated figure.

Warners would never have a better team player, or so constant a troublemaker. He was enough of a radical to grumble at the slave labor at the studio. He loathed Jack because he felt underpaid and overworked. It was years before he got up to a salary level—$3,000 a week—such as Robinson (and Dick Powell!) enjoyed. He was always threatening to strike or quit, with his brother Bill, the tough guy in the family, acting as his manager or enforcer. He did cross over to Grand National for two pictures, duds, made in imitation of his Warners movies. But then he came back on a better deal and stayed there until the early forties. He was the Mick rebel who called Jack the *shvontz*—the prick—and meant it, but he had the heart of a family loyalist.[9]

Just a few months after *Little Caesar*, April 23, 1931, *The Public Enemy* opened. It was always a better film than *Little Caesar*, but it was another hit, a wind in which every would-be talent wanted to flutter. Darryl Zanuck always claimed that he had purchased Cagney and Joan Blondell, and whatever play it was they were in, for the studio. Maybe. The play was *Maggie the Magnificent*, and it closed after thirty-two performances in New York. But two people got rave notices in it, Cagney and Blondell. This was 1929 (*Maggie* opened the night of the Crash): he was thirty; she was twenty-three. He had been acting, and dancing on stage; she had been in vaudeville. Someone asked her what she did there, and she said, "Oh, honey, everything but my laundry."[10] These pretty kids talked like hard-boiled ruffians.

The couple were teamed again in another play, *Penny Arcade*, and that's when Al Jolson saw them. So he bought the play and sold it to Warners, on the condition that Cagney and Blondell would appear on screen in the film of *Penny Arcade*—that turned out as *Sinners' Holiday* (1930), though the newcomers were dropped into minor roles. So they had been shipped out to California and they were waiting, but not entirely appreciated, because they were Jolson protégés, and even Jack was nervous of high-hatting Al.

As the feeling for crime pictures began to spread, two Warners writers, Kubec Glasmon and John Bright, fashioned what they called a novel in manuscript. It was titled "Beer and Blood," and it promised a gangster film in which two slum kids grow up—one becomes a real hoodlum, while his pal is a more easygoing guy.

Zanuck and Jack Warner liked the "novel" once they were

spared the chore of reading by having the writers pitch it. Glasmon and Bright thought Cagney would be good in it. He had already done *Doorway to Hell* at the studio, in which Lew Ayres played the gangster boss—that gentle actor would do a lot of good work, but he was no one's gangster. Zanuck agreed, and said that Cagney should be the sidekick, with Edward Woods as Tom Powers, the true motor for the project. William Wellman was assigned to direct.

Then something happened that helps explain Warners, the movies, and Cagney. Wellman was an experienced director, confident with tough male roles and action scenes. Working at Paramount, he had directed *Wings* (1927), a flying picture from the Great War that had won the first Best Picture Oscar.

But something troubled him as "Beer and Blood" got under way. After a few days, Wellman was looking at the early footage with his cutter and he felt uneasy without knowing why. Then he got it. He realized they had the casting wrong. Edward Woods was too restrained in the lead role, Tom Powers, while Cagney was seething with unused energy as Matt Doyle.

Wellman called Zanuck, who was in New York, and explained the dilemma. Zanuck did not believe in doubt: he was devout about immediate decisions. "Make the switch," he ordered, which would mean later on that he took credit for it.[11] Woods lingered a few years until Warners dropped him. During the war, he made training films with Ronald Reagan. But Jimmy became Cagney.

The Public Enemy is seventy-four minutes long, and it tells the story of a kid who becomes a civic monster and a dark star. In comparison, you do feel that Edward G. Robinson was rather condescending over the chance to play a bad man and a flagrant ham. Cagney commits to the film, and is so unpredictable that there is no room for ham. Tom Powers is a force, warned about his destiny by his mother and brother. He shoots people in the back. He treats women as trophies or bores. He deserves the condemnation in the film's title. But in the face of his zest, that title is too half-hearted to ponder what "the Public" might mean. The picture sold out when it opened because the humbug of American virtue had been dumped like an inconvenient corpse. As Kenneth Tynan put it, much later, Cagney "presented for the first time, a hero who was callous and evil, while being simultaneously equipped with charm, courage and a sense of fun. In one stroke Cagney abolished both the convention of the pure hero and that of approximate equipoise between vice and virtue."[12]

Of course, Tom Powers has to die, but only after the tour de force of Cagney's staggering cadenza in the pouring rain. Gangsters enjoy magnificent endings—get ready for *Bonnie and Clyde*. Death is Powers's last great act, like King Kong on top of the Empire State Building—and those two rogues are equally out of control yet secure in our hearts. I don't mean to suggest that Jack Warner, Zanuck, Wellman, and Cagney sat down and worked this out. Still, *The Public Enemy* is an anarchist exultation in which "law and order" is a forlorn concession to what we are supposed to think. Here we are, in 1931, at a time of devastated economy and diminishing hope, with an inspiring celebration of outlawry. Warner Bros is often thanked for its liberal sentiments and social concerns. But that is hogwash if you really inhabit Cagney's energy in *The Public Enemy*. We are witnessing, and enjoying, a force of unhindered danger. That people demanded to see it was a sign of how the movies had uncovered our violence and despair.

All of which leads to the most notorious thing in the film. Tom Powers the mobster has a mistress, named Kitty, played by Mae Clarke. There is a breakfast scene: he is tousled, in pajamas; she wears a housecoat. It is plain that they have slept together, without much pleasure. Aggravated by her chatter, Tom picks up a half grapefruit and rams it in her face. Censorship passed this (though Will Hays was unhappy with the film), and there are viewers still who cheer and laugh at it, no matter that Kitty has done nothing to merit the attack. She has not betrayed Tom; she has not stolen from him; she has not even talked back to him. There is no back story beyond her and the grapefruit's availability and Cagney's restless need to do something and be somebody—to behave as if in a movie.

Zanuck said *he* had thought of the grapefruit; he dreamed it up in a script conference. But later on, the abused Mae Clarke supported Wellman's claim that it had been *his* idea. The director admitted that he had not much liked the actress's face, while being reminded of regrets over the third marriage on which he had just embarked. Others said it was folklore from some real gangster's career. Mae Clarke regretted the incident: "I'm sorry I ever agreed to do the grapefruit bit. I never dreamed it would be shown in the movie." There is even the chance—you can feel this on screen—that Wellman just told Cagney to do it without letting Ms. Clarke in on "the joke."[13]

Here is a movie where men are slaughtered so casually we don't keep count. But the grapefruit seems to smack our own faces. The scene hurts, and it disparages women as a whole. If the fruit had been used against Jean Harlow, who plays a cool society woman drawn to Tom's danger, I suspect that shock would have been cut, because beauty and class were being assaulted and they were sacrosanct, whereas Ms. Clarke's Kitty is seen as a drab and a nag.

There's one more version that feels more reliable. It comes from John Bright, co-writer on *The Public Enemy*. The grapefruit was always in the script, he said, but Mae Clarke came to work that day with a bad cold, so she asked Cagney to go easy on her sore nose. The actor agreed, but when Wellman heard about their arrangement, he grabbed the gentlemanly actor. "Fuck her nose," he said. "If it's real, this scene will make you one of the biggest stars in the business. You give it to her, really give it to her."

The actor pondered, and did it full force—you can see Clarke's pain, *and* her hurt at the broken pact. As soon as "Cut!" was called, she belted Cagney in the face and called him a "double-crossing Irish no-good." Then she slapped Bright, too —it's his story.[14]

Poor Kitty is a sign of how little patience the Warners gangster films had for women. Jean Harlow looks interesting for a moment with Cagney, but then we recall how seldom he risked love stories on screen. That prospect was the one thing to still his energy—though his shy bemusement can be pleasing in a picture like *The Strawberry Blonde*, where his Biff Grimes (Cagney names are like jabs in boxing) is suspended between Rita Hayworth and Olivia de Havilland. One day on the set of *The Public Enemy* Harlow passed by and Cagney noticed her upright breasts. He kidded her about how she kept them that way. "I'm just going to ice 'em," said Harlow.[15] If only the film had more of that sparring.

But the idea of a prize dame for a rising hoodlum was strictly theoretical in the thirties—as late as the Al Pacino *Scarface* (1983), Tony scrambles to woo the sexy but cold Elvira (Michelle Pfeiffer), then promptly loses interest in her. In *Little Caesar*, as has been noted, Rico is hostile to women from the start. There are even interpretations that his character is gay. That's a stretch for 1931, but it's a sign of how thoroughly the studio neglected female characters. This is enough to prepare you for the great battles fought by Bette Davis (who was another kind of emotional intimidator, and who rarely took prisoners).

When Jack Warner talked about that grapefruit sequence, he managed to make it seem like a marketing strategy:

> This brutal bit of business achieved a kind of grisly immortality, aroused endless resentment among militant feminists [Jack wrote this in 1965] and made "Czar" Will Hays stew in

the office where he was being paid a huge salary to protect the movies from that sort of attack. I have no doubt that innumerable young lovers, discovering that their sweeties got a masochistic delight watching this rough stuff, adopted the grapefruit technique to get what they wanted. It may have been hard on Hollywood in particular and stubborn girls in general, but it sure was great for the grapefruit business.[16]

Facetiousness allied to cynicism: it's the cocky attitude ready to trump Einstein on relativity. Just two years later, in the very funny *Hard to Handle*, Cagney plays a con artist who promotes marathon dance contests . . . and a craze for grapefruit! Warner Bros knew just what they were doing—and they wanted us to know, too. It's a sign of the cheerful battle Warners (and every other studio) fought with censorship or high-minded theories of responsibility over gangster violence. There's a brazen amorality that runs riot in *Little Caesar* and *The Public Enemy*. The sense of abandon is a little like the earliest rock and roll. In the same *Hard to Handle* (directed by Mervyn LeRoy), Cagney says the public is a cow that needs to be milked. That was us! And audiences were laughing at the jab.

Will Hays was indignant over gangster films. Howard Hughes made his *Scarface* (on a much bigger budget) just as *Little Caesar* and *The Public Enemy* (cost $150,000, ice included) were being made. Hays opposed *Scarface* and delayed its release until 1932. More than that, he imposed a subtitle on the project, "Shame of the Nation," and required a scene where civic leaders and newspaper people discuss gangsterism and lecture us on what a terrible thing it is. (Director Howard Hawks kept this scene so flat he hoped audiences would guess it was an add-on to all the elegant scenes of slaughter.)

The public suffered such reservations, and interpreted them as humbug from a business that would do anything it could to sell tickets. The humble upstart who seizes power was a very winning fantasy—it matched the ascent of people like the Warners, who had gained social heights without education, class privilege, or old family money, and without abandoning the aura of eastern European Jewry. And all of this was happening at a moment when so many Americans were without the money to survive. So bromides rang out, and quite soon, with the coming of the Production Code, gangster films lost their rough edge. Cagney started to play hoodlums and rascals for laughs—and in time he became a hard-bitten, punchy gangster (Flicker Hayes) with Blondell as his ex-hooker sweetheart (*He Was Her Man*); a daredevil self-destructive (*The Crowd Roars, Ceiling Zero*); or on the side of the law itself, as "Brick" Davis in *G Men*. That gentrification of the gangster spirit would find its most unexpected hero in Humphrey Bogart, who in the thirties was just one of the small-part dirty rats Cagney had to dispose of.

Some of the wishful bromides came from honest hearts and citizens in Hollywood who donated to charity and did good works, no matter that their profits came from so many kinds of exploitation. At the time of *The Public Enemy*, the solemn Harry Warner—who reproved his stars if they sexually harassed secretaries said, "Gangster pictures are not responsible for the wildness of youth, nor are there too many gangster pictures. . . . Gangster pictures properly presented should have a good effect. They are intended to point out the lesson that crime does not pay. With proper home training, they should assist in keeping kids from turning into delinquents."[17]

You can see Jack's grin and the swagger that urged, "You tell 'em, Harry! Give 'em hell."

Bette Davis in *The Letter*—hated nearly every minute at Warners and made it fit for dangerous women

12

Bette v. Everyone

IT OFFENDED HIS BROTHER Harry, but Jack Warner had a clear-cut attitude toward females: there were those you married, and those you played around with. Don't let them get confused. This worked, if you were in America, careless of old family attitudes, and if you were rich enough to pay the bills. To be "somebody" was a license to be out of control in the fresh fields of violence and sex.

Harry thought Jack's policy lacked tact or taste; it was letting the family down. But Jack had another theory: that a guy in the audience often had his girl with him—a wife or a date—and he was solid about that tie. But that didn't stop him dreaming about all the other pretty women Busby Berkeley had up on screen for one of his haremlike routines. The essential arrangement of all movies—our dark and their light—was to legitimize or condone fantasy. This could seem pretty, but it was a formula for sexism, a motif that would one day help undermine the American movie.

Joan Blondell was a case in point. I have made the claim already that she is the soul of one of the finest moments in Warners history, singing "Remember My Forgotten Man" in *Gold Diggers of 1933*, where the song is entrusted to her. She could sing, she could dance, she could handle a joke, be sexy, obedient, a pal. She did whatever was required, and didn't ask the system for more. She had come to Warners with Cagney: they played together seven times, and their mutual fondness is plain. He said he'd have married her, if he wasn't tied up already—not every star was so restrained. Jimmy the agitator was always goading Joan to fight for a better contract—and she was paid a fraction of what Cagney earned. But she resisted the advice; she really was as easygoing as she seemed on screen. She was the one girl who liked Jack Warner, and she did her bit, even during long shooting days when she was pregnant. She appreciated being at Warners; she had a feeling for a worthwhile show being put on for the crowd:

> I related to shopgirls and chorus girls, just ordinary gals who were hoping. I would get endless fan mail from girls saying "That is exactly what I would have done, if I'd been in your shoes, you did exactly the right thing." So I figured that was my popularity, relating to the girls. They just wanted more of the same thing. All you got were new clothes and new sets, but the stories were pretty much alike and I was the same type. But those early days of talkies were incredible, what with the soundproof camera booth and everything, I think that's why they signed Cagney and me so fast, 'cause we just went through it like we were on a stage and they weren't used to that. We were showing something different, something fast and to the point.[1]

The only bad fan mail Blondell received was when word got out that she had married Dick Powell in life—the actual shopgirls of America took it for granted that Dick must be married to his screen sweetie, Ruby Keeler. That was Joan's second marriage. The first was to cameraman George Barnes (1933–36), who shot *Footlight Parade* and *He Was Her Man*, among many others. At Warners, she married within the studio family. Her passion, she said, would be number 3, Mike Todd (1947–50)— that was before he married Elizabeth Taylor (who hadn't been born yet when Joan was signed by Warners).

Blondell was at Warners all through the thirties, and she had star rating, but no really prominent parts. Take *Stage Struck*, a Busby Berkeley film from 1936, made during her marriage to Dick Powell (1936–44). Blondell plays Peggy Revere, the lead in a new Broadway show that George Randall (Powell) is producing. She is also the show's financial backer. But Powell is really soft on a younger, superior dancer (played by Jeanne Madden); Peggy is dropped and the kid gets her break. Madden had caught Jack Warner's eye—she made just three films and ended up running a boarding house in Pennsylvania. Jack's eye had neither memory nor conscience, but Blondell went on, year after year.

She rose as high as a chorus girl could go, playing what she called "whore-ladies," who somehow knew much more about life than Joan. But Warners also had an instinct for lady-ladies, witness their promotion of Kay Francis. Francis is not well known today, and a lot of her work has dated badly. But her career needs to be understood as it worked in the 1930s, and it runs counter to the orthodoxy that Warners had no interest in women. Francis was from Oklahoma and a hard-luck showbiz family, but she always carried herself as ladylike. She had dark hair, soulful if not mournful eyes, and a rather pursed mouth that was maybe anxious over her genteel lisp. You only have to see her in Lubitsch's *Trouble in Paradise* (at Paramount) to recognize her wit and her mischief. She might have gone in other directions.

But in 1932, Warners made a deal with agent Myron Selznick to take on her and William Powell as a sophisticated couple. Together, she and Powell made hits out of *One Way Passage* and *Jewel Robbery*. In *One Way Passage*, Joan Ames (Francis) has a terminal illness and Dan Hardesty (Powell) is a convicted murderer. They meet on an ocean liner, the site of a doomed floating romance. As directed by Tay Garnett and scripted by Wilson Mizner and Joseph Jackson, it is as hokey as it is effective. Francis had trademarks: a sad smile and an expensive wardrobe. Female audiences responded with regularity, and even if she was hardly in the Warners tradition, the studio paid her better than any other actress—her salary went as high as $5,000 a week. In *Jewel Robbery* (which is very close to *Trouble in Paradise*), Francis is a baroness with jewels and a wandering eye, and Powell is the gentleman thief who romances her. Powell soon moved away to MGM, but Francis became a Warners fixture.

She was as dependent on her clothes (by Orry-Kelly) as she was on scenarios that never doubted her romantic appeal. She was sometimes a professional woman—*Mary Stevens, M.D.*, and *The White Angel* (in which she played Florence Nightingale). But she could stretch: she was a onetime prostitute trying to go straight in *Mandalay*; in *I Found Stella Parish* she is a famous actress with a guilty secret, on another ocean voyage; in *Stolen Holiday*, she is a fashion model who helps a rascal Claude Rains in his investment schemes; in *Confession* she is a famous singer who had a secret affair; and in *The First Lady* she is a woman who tries to seek the presidential nomination for her husband (played by Preston Foster).

This is a selection from more than twenty films she did at Warners. Kay Francis was practical about her status: she made a lot of money doing rather silly "Kay Fwancis" pictures. She wore the clothes and seldom caused trouble until at last she talked of suing the studio for mistreatment. That seems to have soured Jack Warner. She was one of a group of stars written off as box office poison (Katharine Hepburn and Garbo were others), and she was approaching forty. She was dropped at the very point when she was being considered for the dying Judith Traherne in *Dark Victory*—which was a Francis-type vehicle, until Bette Davis took charge of it. Francis left Warners, and Davis inherited her dressing room. And Davis is more important to this history than Cagney, just as she was a more radical screen presence.

There were times when Bette Davis lamented how fate had led her to Warner Bros, to Jack Warner and Hal Wallis, to a creative climate beset by male chauvinism. If only she had been elsewhere? I think that notion is humbug. Bette was looking for a battle, whether she could know that, or admit it. At any other studio, she would have become a problem, because her angry eyes needed to feel she was embattled and scorned. There are artistic spirits that can be crushed by kindness and understanding.

In which case, Davis was at exactly the right studio, where the battle lines would be drawn up early, and held to despite her success. Jack Warner was always of the opinion that Bette was neither pretty nor sexy—but where would she have been without that doubt? Even Hal Wallis once admitted to her that while he admired what she had done, at a personal level he really didn't like her pictures.

All that outsider managed was two Oscars, nominations for Best Actress five times in a row in Hollywood's richest era, and a lot of money made for Warner Bros on a string of films that can still be watched today with pleasure and surprise. And if she wasn't simply pretty or sexy, maybe that was more radical than the allure of Cagney's intimations of outrage. Jimmy and Bette were fellow marauders—rapists, nearly, to tender sentimentality—and the irony is that when they were put together on screen (*Jimmy the Gent* and *The Bride Came C.O.D.*), it just didn't work. Cagney was too polite, or intimidated, and Bette was too admiring or restrained. They both needed to be opposed. They were at the right studio, at home. (But just imagine her as Ma in *White Heat*, with a moaning Jimmy on her lap.)

The most important men in Bette's screen life are those she loses, gives up, triumphs over, or kills. Like Judith Traherne, about to go out of focus at the end of *Dark Victory*, she doesn't want to be disturbed. Show Bette a happy ending and she could really get nasty.

The very first words of Davis's rueful memoir, *The Lonely Life* (1962), put us on alert: "I have always been driven by some distant music—a battle hymn no doubt—for I have been at war from the beginning."[2] She was from Lowell, Massachusetts, born in 1908, the daughter of a lawyer who left the family when she was a child. That put her very close to her mother, who was not just her best adviser but a real friend. She loved movies—Valentino and Mary Pickford—and then she lost her heart to the stage. It was only after sound had arrived that she found herself in Hollywood.

She would tell stories later about how she had to try to be sexy for moguls and auditions, and how horrifying that was. We tell stories to get through; she changed her name from Betty to Bette, a tiny touch but typical. You can have an absorbing time looking at her early work trying to decide whether she was pretty, or not. Or what the hell was it about her? She was slim, with full breasts and a walk that had an odd writhe to it; she could go very blonde in those days, and that was striking in black and white. Then she reacted so fast she seemed hungry or threatened. She looked at men with a suspicion close to contempt, and when she spoke it was not just Boston, but elocution, refinement along with insolence. At the same time, she believed in manners while being quite rude. This hoodlum pose was seductive. She could have played Lady Bracknell at twenty-three and changed your sense of that play. Graham Greene remarked on her "corrupt and phosphorescent prettiness."[3]

She did a few things at Universal, where one boss said she

was only as sexy as Slim Summerville (a homely character actor). Later on, she would claim she was about to give up when the veteran English actor George Arliss picked her to play with him in *The Man Who Played God* at Warners. He was listened to at Warners, because his *Disraeli* had won him the Best Actor Oscar in 1930. Perhaps it took an older, sadder man to see that this twenty-four-year-old was so needy yet so smart you didn't quite appreciate her fierce vulnerability. Warners signed her to a five-year contract that would run for eighteen. Jack Warner soon discovered she was a pain in the neck, but she was determined to stay their pain.

In terms of credentials and education, Davis was closer to a lady than the Kay Francis who joined the studio at the same time. But Francis was comfortable, to the point of languor, at being someone men thought they wanted. Bette never fell for that. She was outspoken, intelligent, and her own lawyer—she had agents, et cetera, but she never trusted the job to them.

For a few years she was put in a lot of minor films, but she was very noticeable in *The Cabin in the Cotton*, telling a staid Richard Barthelmess that she'd kiss him, but "I just washed my hair." Then she was cast opposite Spencer Tracy (the only time they worked together) in *20,000 Years in Sing Sing*, and they had a chemistry that a smarter studio might have jumped on. Soon after that she did *Jimmy the Gent*, sparring with Cagney.

Bette was already seen as a shameless self-promoter at Warners—just look at her wrathful, searching gaze and compare it with the doelike trust of Joan Blondell. It was part of Bette's awareness of the world beyond Burbank that she heard RKO was planning to make Somerset Maugham's *Of Human Bondage*, and knew she was born to play Mildred, the vicious tart who ruins the life of the hero. She had read the book, not something many actresses could claim. Warners was against the idea: Mildred was such a brazen bitch, any actress going near her was bound to earn lasting public loathing. They never realized how that risk was gravy for Bette. So she nagged and haggled, with Maugham's backing, and in the end she got the part, with John Cromwell directing and Leslie Howard playing the sorrowful, clubfooted Philip Carey.

Of Human Bondage is a harsh story, and Maugham never bothered to like Mildred. But in 1934, Hollywood was squeamish about doing her justice. At a key point, Davis overruled the studio makeup people and said that she would determine the look for Mildred. "I made it pretty clear that Mildred was not going to die of a dread disease looking as if a deb had missed her noon nap."[4] (There was never any doubt that Davis wrote *The Lonely Life* herself.)

She is lurid and scary in *Of Human Bondage*, not only in terms of the ravaged appearance—she looks like someone just out of a bad hospital—but because of her commitment to the ruthless mindset of Mildred. Davis did say she was alarmed at what she'd learned about herself in the process. Actresses played whores who ended badly sometimes, but in a veiled, cosmetic way that retained their star glamour. When Garbo dies as *Camille* there's a tasteful cough, but little more damage. As Mildred, Bette feels infectious and so desperate that Leslie Howard becomes a stricken and pale onlooker. He nearly faints at one moment because of her vileness. It is an intense performance and a recasting of the original novel. Philip is no longer the central character he was meant to be.

Swept along by conviction, Bette believed she had actually been nominated for her performance. That was not so: many Academy members were too horrified by Mildred to be appreciative. But a groundswell developed to make Davis a write-in candidate. That gesture was permitted, and then rescinded; the Academy has its own code of correctness. The prize went to Claudette Colbert, lovely, cool, and amusing in *It Happened One Night*, but that was only kindling for the fire in Bette's eyes that she had been wronged.

This raging victim returned to Warners, and as she saw it, she was back on a diet of mediocre films and halfhearted parts. She was correct in most respects. Warners did not know how to use her, and there was still a feeling that she was an upstart, a know-all, and her own worst enemy—that triple threat in women who speak their mind and treat male condescension with derision. Still, Bette herself did not quite understand the potential in *Dangerous*, a Warners project for 1935.

As written by Laird Doyle, and directed by Alfred E. Green (at a mere seventy-nine minutes), *Dangerous* is an offbeat picture. Franchot Tone plays a successful young architect, Don Bellows, about to be married. But then he runs across Joyce Heath (Davis), the wreck of a once promising actress. Bette was still only twenty-eight, and she never looked better, but Joyce has the fatalistic edge of a self-destructive. The role was said to be based on the real Jeanne Eagels. Don falls for Joyce and tries to revive her career. But she is married already, to an abject failure, and that has drawn her into self-pity and alcoholism. Still, she is about to resume acting, because of Don's love; but then she turns against herself and abandons her new play. Don accuses her of self-centeredness. Close to suicide, she heeds a tougher lesson—live in reality instead of melodrama. So she determines to own up to her marriage, to forsake Don, and to do what she can as an actress. She is alone. As Bette was meant to be.

No one seems to have anticipated what *Dangerous* could become, but the casual approach let pathos and desperation breathe. Bette did not think much of the picture herself—she turned it down at first. She did develop a crush on Franchot Tone, who was then engaged to Joan Crawford. But the acting community was in shame over how Bette had been deprived of anything for *Of Human Bondage*, so she won a kind of sympathy Oscar for *Dangerous*. The resolution of its story is close to hysteria, but the portrait of a chronic actress with mixed feelings about acting is intriguing—the film could play well with Ingmar Bergman's *Persona* (1966). The Oscar was as deserved as any acting prize ever is, and even Warners had to admit that her status was raised.

She hoped her path was clear now, but the studio put her in a dismal version of *The Maltese Falcon*, titled *Satan Met a Lady*, playing opposite Warren William. Next, she was told to play a lumberjack in a film to be called *God's Country and the Woman*. (Titles that isolated the female were often a sign of sexist indifference.) She protested to Jack Warner himself, and he told her, "Just be a good girl and everything will work out."[5] He even dangled the possibility of *Gone With the Wind* in front of her. That novel had just been published in 1936, and it was unclear what would happen to it. But Davis declined to be a lumberjack, and she was put on suspension. Whereupon she devised another kind of movie for herself, a public melodrama, in which a headstrong actress would challenge her stupid employer.

Ludovic Toeplitz, a European producer, had invited her to do two pictures on the Continent. What a clever and provocative way to work off her suspension. She knew that Warners would move to stop this plan. So she sailed secretly to England to avoid being served with injunctions. It was in London, at Claridge's Hotel, that she received the legal charges—this was a better script than either of the planned European films, and it led to a court case in which a naughty, spoiled actress or a victim of a modern slave trade would be sued by a righteously aggrieved employer or a callous factory system. (Take your pick.)

Sir Patrick Hastings and Sir William Jowitt were the star lawyers in court. The matter dominated the press for days, and everyone in the picture business was taking sides. Bette and Jack Warner both gave testimony in a case the actress was bound to lose—except in the eye of publicity and public opinion, and its general estimate that Hollywood was a cruel place. I think all parties guessed the outcome, and maybe once or twice Jack was shrewd enough to see that Bette was running this movie. (He covered the event in less than a page in his self-glorious auto-biography; Bette gave it eleven in hers.)[6]

Warners won. The actress had her "inhuman bondage" (her words) stretched out to 1942. "I was exhausted. This defeat was a real blow to me," she wrote. "It was a one hundred per cent defeat."[7] Not everyone saw it that way. George Arliss, still a friend, told her, "Go back and face them proudly." She did so, and her supremacy began. Jack had been trounced in his victory. He agreed that Warners would share the hefty damages levied against her by the British court. He welcomed the prodigal home.

Her parts and her pictures picked up. In *Marked Woman*, she played a whore beaten up by the mob but still ready to testify for a district attorney based on Thomas Dewey, but played by Humphrey Bogart. Yet again she shocked the makeup department by doing her own slashed face. In *Kid Galahad*, a boxing movie, she was "Fluff," girlfriend to Edward G. Robinson's trainer. But there was still serious talk about *Gone With the Wind*.

Davis was imperious: "It was insanity that I not be given Scarlett. But then, Hollywood has never been rational."[8] David O. Selznick had been laboring with the best-selling Margaret Mitchell novel. He had a script that was a prelude to rewrites. He was testing anyone and everyone for Scarlett (but not Bette), and he needed money. He devised two ways to go: make a deal with Warners, for Bette as Scarlett and Errol Flynn as Rhett; or go to his father-in-law, Louis B. Mayer, at MGM, get Clark Gable for Rhett, get some money, and cross his fingers for a Scarlett. Bette doubted Flynn could play Rhett, but the decision was out of her hands. Selznick went with family, so then Jack Warner demonstrated his opportunistic cheek by intervening with his own southern belle picture, *Jezebel*. He could taunt Selznick *and* satisfy Bette.

This is New Orleans instead of Georgia, but Julie Marsden

is an unbridled force of reckless, romantic endangerment and risk taking. She offends decorum and her would-be husband Pres (Henry Fonda) by wearing a red dress to a formal ball— this is a black-and-white film, but Bette makes you believe in her scarlet. Too arrogant to apologize, she loses her man. She provokes a duel in which her brother is killed. In the end, as yellow fever mounts, Julie finesses Fonda's bland wife and herself goes to the swamp-ridden quarantine island to take care of Pres in what will be a fatal mission for both of them. Julie persuades the wife that Julie herself must go to the island because she needs to redeem her bad behavior, but we feel how much she wants the exultation of death and glory. This is not wholesome, or even credible, but it happens before our eyes. It's hard to think of a stronger or more willful fantasy for a self-sacrificing emotional tyrant. William Wyler directed, and he was the most careful guide she had worked with—they would have an affair. Before a foot of film had been shot on *Gone With the Wind*, Bette had delivered the performance that would win her second Oscar.[9]

Jezebel is the first film in which Davis's histrionic energy takes over a narrative and plunges it into madness. You can say that the film assumes that women can be crazy in their emotions, but in terms of wish fulfilment the story is as vital to the audience as it is to Bette Davis. For it shows a woman's desire reaching to the point of self-destruction. At last, a woman is saying there are more potent things than the scheme of "happiness" that men have laid out for her. Scarlett lives for another day to exercise her selfishness, but Julie goes up in flames and lights the match herself. Cagney would find that transcendent self-immolation eleven years later in *White Heat*.

A new pattern was set in which Bette made what were clearly Bette Davis films. They're not all good, or plausible, but she had realized intuitively that there was an audience ready to believe in her. All of a sudden, Warners was making women's pictures in which women were in charge.

It's a varied list, with hit after hit. *Dark Victory* was a play that had failed with Tallulah Bankhead, about a woman facing death from a brain tumor. Selznick had thought of it for Garbo. Bette knew it was meant for her—"my favorite, and the public's favorite part I have ever played."[10] In the end, Warners secured the rights and let Bette loose on Judith Traherne. In *Juarez*, she was the Empress Carlotta going mad, as her life and her Mexican empire came apart. In *The Old Maid*, she went to makeup and painful self-effacement to be a spinster who must watch over her own daughter as an apparent aunt. In *The Private Lives of Elizabeth and Essex*, she orders the execution of her lover (Errol Flynn). In *All This and Heaven Too*, in France and in period costume, she is a governess who falls in love with the children's father (Charles Boyer).

Then comes *The Letter*, a return to Somerset Maugham's bitter view of women. Leslie Crosbie is the wife of a rubber plantation owner in Malaya, a weak, unobservant fellow well played by Herbert Marshall. As the film opens, she puts six bullets in the body of a man she and her husband had known socially. She will claim he was harassing her, that he meant to rape her, but in fact the couple had had an affair and he was dropping her. She murders him in a fury of rebuffed passion. There is the formality of a trial, though it is assumed in the genteel colonial society that Mrs. Crosbie must be an innocent victim. But then her lawyer (played subtly by James Stephenson) begins to work out the true story and uncover the wickedness in Leslie—which does not stop him being drawn to her.

William Wyler directed what is one of the finest Warners melodramas. Bette is effectively restrained as Leslie; she trusts the duplicity in the role. This is one of her least likable characters, yet she is riveting both sexually and as a person facing her own corruption. Yes, it is a small melodrama, dependent on atmospheric night scenes and a faith in vengeance, lust, and lying. But the script (by Howard Koch) is unrelenting, and the film shows what an intelligent actress Bette was, and how fully in her element in a role that had little in the way of glamour or distracting clothes. The film has a stealth and a confidence that reminds us how, in a time of imminent war, Warner Brothers and other Hollywood studios could muster the resources and the calm to make nearly jubilant studies of human corruption.

Wyler and Davis argued sometimes. She felt she could not say the line "I still love the man I killed" to her husband's face. But Wyler insisted and she did it, and when she described it later you learn a lot about the body of her pictures:

> Yes, I lost a battle, but I lost it to a genius. So many directors were such weak sisters that I would have to take over. Uncreative, unsure of themselves, frightened to fight back, they offered me none of the security that this tyrant did. When working, Willie—like me—could be asked, "Whom do you hate today?" There is always something to fight in this most imperfect of worlds. Creation is hell![11]

That's not a sentiment one would hear from Jack Warner, from Cagney, or from many people in that Hollywood. But Bette could look at other people and at the world so that you appreciate the nature of iniquity and desire. Leslie Crosbie is an ordinary, nasty Englishwoman bored in an outpost of empire. But she is not surprised by evil.

Bette Davis was still only thirty-two. She was not just a star but a dominating figure at Warners. She had beaten the system. Still to come at her home studio were *Now, Voyager* (a popular hit) and *Mr. Skeffington*, in which her unlikability verges on the ideological, as she plays a ruthless, selfish woman cruel and indifferent to her (Jewish) husband (Claude Rains). This woman falls ill and loses her beauty—the director of the film, Vincent

Sherman, was shocked at Bette's zeal with ugly makeup. He warned her that she looked hideous, and she told him off: "My audience likes to see me do this kind of thing."[12]

Davis was loaned out to Goldwyn to do *The Little Foxes*, with Wyler directing again. We may judge in hindsight that her unpleasant characters made better films than the virtuous ones. It was possible to see that her movie looks were going, and after the war she suddenly seemed older. She was still only forty-two when she made *All About Eve* (at Fox), but she looked fifty. It's possible that Bette was too proud to take as much care of herself as other actresses. You wonder whether she even noticed the need.

13

Contracts and Company

LOOKED AT FROM TODAY'S STANCE, there is something unaccountable in the awesome career of Bette Davis. She played queens and empresses from history, and burning icons from modern romance. She was one of the most famous names and images in the world. At her own studio, she was a bit like the unpredictable gunslinger in town. No one wanted to get on the wrong side of Bette, or upset her, because she had made a famous melodrama out of her battle with the studio. That was in the past, but everyone remembered. Even a Jack Warner admitted that Bette had achieved her own way and her own destiny. She had become a force, too smart to realize how crazy she could seem. So in December 1940, she wrote a letter to "Dear Jack":

> I have also heard rumors that *Skeffington* . . . was my next. This, I would be forced for my own future career, to refuse. It is *physically* impossible for me to play this woman of fifty—

I am not old enough in face or figure, and I have worked too hard to do something that I know I would never be convincing in. . . .

If your action in these matters is suspension, or if you decide to give me my three months vacation for next year in January, February and March, I would appreciate knowing as soon as possible so I can open my house in New Hampshire.[1]

We don't know Jack's reply. Maybe he sighed about that incessant Bette and let a couple of years pass. By 1943, she was shooting *Mr. Skeffington* and insisting on her own makeup to the cost of attractiveness. She was terrific in the film, at $5,000 or so a week. But she never earned a penny more from that hit picture; she never knew a residual; and while she often angled for or against certain parts for herself, she hardly ever stepped back from the Warners situation and told herself, be a queen: find a project you love, make it and produce it yourself, and take the profit. Just once, on *A Stolen Life* (1946), she was a secret producer on a picture, as well as playing hostile twin sisters who compete for Glenn Ford—that old sibling rivalry theme. The film did well enough, but she never tried control again.

There were other ways of doing things. Olivia de Havilland was only eight years younger than Bette, but she seemed to be from a next generation. She started in pictures as a teenager and was as pretty as anyone had ever been in a placid or obedient mode. That came from a friendly, modest personality that shone out of her face. She was as well educated as Bette and as intelligent, but it was part of her strategy that she chose to get along with people. As time would determine, she was a very good actress, but in her early days with Warners, she accepted the life of a screen consort. Screenwriter Rowland Leigh petitioned Hal Wallis over the forthcoming *The Charge of the Light Brigade*, with Errol Flynn. Wallis had thought of Anita Louise for the female lead. Wasn't she irrevocably American, Leigh asked. Whereas Olivia de Havilland, "both in looks and voice could, with careful handling, easily be accepted as a young English woman of the Victorian era."[2] Livvy was a lady at a time when English airs meant a lot in Hollywood.

She became Flynn's lady, on screen. They would be together in seven Warners pictures: *Captain Blood*; *The Charge of the Light Brigade*; *The Adventures of Robin Hood*, in which her Maid Marian is a jewel of early Technicolor; *Dodge City*; *The Private Lives of Elizabeth and Essex*, where she is a lady in waiting who loves Essex; *Santa Fe Trail*; and in *They Died with Their Boots On*, where she plays Mrs. Custer.

You can't see those films without guessing at the actors' real fondness. Flynn claimed a love affair; de Havilland would say it was just love, not consummated. More important, the dangerous reputation that Flynn had in the world, and which he deserved, was soothed to some extent by the apparent loyalty the couple enjoyed on screen, and by the universal feeling that de Havilland was as good and nice as her roles. People sometimes said that Ginger Rogers had brought a touch of sex to Fred Astaire, and de Havilland made a good husband out of Flynn on screen. She was stability in his best pictures, though the actress signed her Warners contract in 1936 for $500 a week while her "husband" was at a much higher salary.

She was patient and considerate, yet artful. It took a good deal of maneuvering, and the friendly offices of Jack Warner's wife, Ann, to get her the part of Melanie in *Gone With the Wind*, and she came away from that production so exhausted that she was not ready for her next assignment at Warners, *Elizabeth and Essex*. There had been a scene on that set where she begged off at the end of a long day. So she wrote a letter of apology to Jack Warner that contrasts effectively with the way Bette treated her boss:

> I know that if you had been present on that set, and had realized my problem, you would have dismissed the company

rather than shoot that scene so late in the day. I know, too, that you understand that an actress, no matter how talented she is, is dependent very seriously upon her appearance & her vitality for the quality of her performance. When those two things leave her, whether it is after five years work or at the end of a day, she has nothing to rely on. And when I make suggestions to anyone at the studio, it is for the good of the whole. . . .

You have a tremendous business to conduct, one that you have built to astounding success & complexity, & your time is not to be wasted with trivialities.[3]

Which actress do you want to have writing your letters? Still, de Havilland felt neglected at her own studio. On loan out to Paramount, she got a Best Actress nomination in Mitchell Leisen's *Hold Back the Dawn*, but she was not being offered demanding parts at Warners. So she was refusing scripts and being suspended. It was the Bette Davis story all over again, except that de Havilland took expert legal advice. Martin Gang looked at the statutes and told her that in the state of California it was illegal for any contract to extend beyond seven years, so that the studio practice of adding on suspension time was not legitimate. De Havilland went to court if Jack Warner could find the time to attend—and she won. It was a decision that changed the contract system for all time, just as the confidence that had once reckoned on seven-year deals was coming to a close. De Havilland was not forgiven or renewed at Warners, and she had a period of two years out of work. Jack had been furious: he had brought this actress "from obscurity to prominence," and $125,000 a picture![4] Bette Davis admitted that "Hollywood actors will for ever be in Olivia's debt." Soon enough, she went over to Paramount and won the Oscar twice in four years for *To Each His Own* and *The Heiress*, with another nomination for *The Snake Pit*.

By the time of *The Heiress*, Hollywood was in convulsions:

the Supreme Court had at last determined that production-distribution companies (Warners included) had to sell off their theatres; television was in prospect; the seven-year contract and the whole atmosphere of company cohesion was falling away. But great stars were beginning to originate and own their pictures.

That change would be vast. In 1984, at the time he made *Tightrope*, I interviewed Clint Eastwood on the Warners lot in Burbank. His production company, Malpaso, had a bungalow suite of offices there. Warners had appointed an amiable executive, Joe Hyams, who was known as "vice president for Clint." This relationship had started in 1971, when Eastwood made *Dirty Harry* for Warners after Frank Sinatra, Burt Lancaster, Steve McQueen, and many others had turned down that role. When Eastwood accepted the part, the picture became a Malpaso production—that was the name of the actor's own company.[5]

After the great hit of *Dirty Harry* (it earned $36 million domestically on a $4 million budget), Malpaso generated the pictures on which Clint variously acted, directed, and produced. Some time after Jack Warner's death, Malpaso would earn two Best Picture Oscars for Warners—*Unforgiven* and *Million Dollar Baby*. These pictures were distributed by Warners and represented an important element in the studio's revenue. So Eastwood was a profit (or loss) participant in what he made. He was an iconic actor, a proficient director, and a great producer. Jack Warner would have applauded him and started telling him awful jokes. For Jack had known and marketed the prototype taciturn hero, John Wayne. Clint had become his own business, and that model has dominated Hollywood now for decades. It is a role that neither Bette Davis nor Jimmy Cagney explored. So for years and contracts they griped about the lousy deal and imperfect attention they were getting from Jack Warner.

Eastwood has been a self-made industry, a model of movie

success in his time, who had graduated from the Universal training school by way of a TV series and Italian westerns to reach
unrivaled authority. And he carried himself like a man who had
expected no less. If he made mistakes, he took the blame—and
sometimes fired people. When he did well, he smiled that Clint
smile on the way to a net worth not far short of $400 million
now. He admired Warners and he knew the studio history. He
had seen some of it happen: Clint is actually a year older than
James Dean would have been; he knew the kid and saw him
come and go.

So Bette Davis was driven to fury over all the bad scripts
sent to her as assignments, and she would never forget how
Jack and Hal Wallis didn't really like her. But there are other
ways of regarding the studio system: you would have to allow
that George Raft refused to do *The Maltese Falcon* with John
Huston because he thought it was not an "important" picture.[6]
Paul Muni declined *High Sierra* because he felt it had no message. Edward G. Robinson was a notorious fusspot who wanted
to change most scripts sent to him—"As I see it, Eddie," Darryl
Zanuck had written to him in 1932, "the whole fault lies in the
fact that you want to be a writer. By this I mean that you want
to put your views into whatever subject we purchase rather
than to accept the views of the men I engage here who are spe-
cialists at a high salary in this specific work."[7] So Eddie declined *Lawyer Man*, and William Powell had a hit with it. Bette
Davis hadn't wanted to do *Dangerous*. And maybe there *was* a
morning when *Casablanca* might have been Hedy Lamarr and
Ronald Reagan. And maybe it would have worked (and changed
his life and our history).

Meanwhile, Bogart and Bergman worked out pretty well.
The studio was against having Dooley Wilson as Sam: "He isn't
ideal for the part," said Hal Wallis, "but if we get stuck and can't
do any better I suppose he could do it."[8] Today, Dooley Wilson
is immortal, even if few recall what became of him. Warners

was a school or a prison, beset by gossip, rumor, lies, and false reports. Everyone wanted to know everyone else's business and talk behind your back. And so, yes, *Casablanca* was made in a state of chaos and disagreement, but within weeks of its opening it was regarded as enchanted. Today, it is axiomatic, a given, something that came down from heaven as a classic benediction on factory moviemaking.

As we know, *Casablanca* was directed by Michael Curtiz, who also directed several films acclaimed in this book: *20,000 Years in Sing Sing, Mandalay, Jimmy the Gent, Captain Blood, The Adventures of Robin Hood,* and *Yankee Doodle Dandy.* Curtiz was not what I would think of calling a "great" director; Andrew Sarris placed him in this "Lightly Likable" category.[9] Everyone told stories about comical things Curtiz would say on set. But no one can look at his pictures without feeling his camera fluency and his grasp of movie moments. The executives at Warners wearied of his doing elaborate, unscripted shots for their own sake, because they seemed eloquent. But they kept him on because his films worked. Lightly Likable is OK, if it persists over thirty years on all manner of films where maybe Curtiz hardly read the scripts. Perhaps he never bothered to read because he knew there'd be a rewrite.

Curtiz was under contract at Warners, just as much as Bogart and other actors, along with the writers and the craftspeople—Owen Marks edited *Casablanca,* and did the same job on *The Petrified Forest, The Treasure of the Sierra Madre,* and *East of Eden;* Arthur Edeson photographed it—as well as *Each Dawn I Die, They Drive by Night,* and *The Maltese Falcon;* Carl Jules Weyl was the art director—as he had been on *Kid Galahad, The Adventures of Robin Hood,* and *The Letter.* Max Steiner wrote the music that was a sauce poured over so many Warners pictures and which came to be the theme music of the entire studio.

We don't have to sentimentalize this company of collaborators and claim they were all friends or even a team. Anyone who has worked in an office for years has met its festering antagonisms. But these people knew each other, the actors and the executives, and they had by heart what you have to call a house style. They worked long days under great pressure. They could be ousted or replaced by sharper talents, or by downright betrayal. But they were paid very well, even at the lower levels, and they were engaged on a project that stirred the public at large. To be making movies during the Depression and the Second World War was to be on the front lines for raising morale. It was to feel you were somebody.

The pictures from Warners, from sound to 1950, were not very flexible. Vehicles made on a production line are resolutely alike. So they repeat the same problems as well as the virtues: most Warners pictures were moody, fast, tough yet romantic, gritty but in a stylish way. So many feelings were cast in a dark or sardonic light—long before film noir was recognized. They also had narrow theories on men and women, happy endings, honor, courage, and race—and those principles have proved too fixed or conservative for a developing America. You shouldn't judge Warners in those years by, say, *M*, *La Règle du Jeu*, *L'Atalante*, or *Bicycle Thieves*. It's not even legitimate to test Warners' product against *The Shop Around the Corner*, *Citizen Kane*, or *His Girl Friday*—American vehicles that drove in new, contrarian ways. You can't usefully measure a Warners picture against what was being done by Edward Hopper, Duke Ellington, or William Faulkner (though Faulkner often worked at Warners). You should admit that the studio was usually short on comedies—yet full of wisecracking. But you risk misunderstanding America in those same years if you don't take into account *I Am a Fugitive from a Chain Gang*, *Gold Diggers of 1933*, *The Adventures of Robin Hood*, *The Letter*, and *Casablanca*. Plus— if you'll wait a bit—you may decide that the movie of *The Big Sleep* was even in a class with Faulkner or Hopper (as well as one of the funniest pictures ever made).

We have long since exhausted the aura of old Hollywood, and there's no reason to romanticize it. The SIGN sits up in the hills above Los Angeles, humorless and archaic, as if pilots didn't know where to land. The romantic attitudes of movies hindered rational thought and social progress—perhaps they curtailed it, for unleashed dreaming stifles evidence. The stereotypes have been a source of damage that we are still trying to repair. Ours is not a tough guy's world—but that dream persists. Still, it's unfair to omit the spirit in which people worked in the factory, when work was denied to so many Americans. No one recalled that spirit better than Joan Blondell—and no one had delivered it better on screen:

> Oh, those musicals were tough. Much tougher than a straight movie. And the hours were awful because we didn't have unions then. We worked any time they wanted to work. You could come in to work at 6:00 a.m. and work till midnight and then be back at 6:00 next morning. And you might have breakfast at 6:30 and then not break for lunch till 3:00 in the afternoon. You'd be ready to fall over. Then you'd work all day Saturday, and they made it a point to work all night Saturday night. It was awfully tough. And I don't think it was like that at all the studios. I think they specialized in it at Warners. They had something hot going for them: the musicals and the gangster things. And they had a bunch of us who were *hot*, and they were going to wring it dry. . . . But at Warners we were all in it together. Happy, sad, well, ill, we all talked to each other. The crew too. The crew was an important part of our life and they were great. We made them happy, they made us happy. It was like, "Okay, guys, we're all tired and exhausted, but we've got a job to do, we've done it before, let's put up the old fight and do it the best we can." We were never afraid to have guts.[10]

14

Unafraid?

SIDE BY SIDE with Joan Blondell, who wouldn't be there at 6:00 a.m.? So the working conditions were tough, and the exploitation was automatic, but even the world-weary tough guys and the dames could respond to the rhetoric of the Warner Bros product. They were doing it for the team, and maybe the team could save the world. Nearly everyone in movies in those days had the dream—from Charlie Chaplin to Jack Warner—that in troubled times the movies were a medium in which we were all together. Adolf Hitler thought exactly the same thing. He loved pictures. I put it that way because it's hard to be a cockeyed optimist unless you have a pack of sour wisecracks to go with the deal.

But the spirit was real and it was braver at Warners than anywhere else. Consider Robert Lord, one of the invaluable middlemen at the studio. He had been a producer on *Gold Diggers of 1933*. He had watched the team do "Remember My Forgotten Man." Maybe he was the one who said, give Blondell that close-up. At exactly the same time, in the spring of 1933, when the money pinch was at its most severe and when Warners agreed to fifty percent pay cuts—that's when Darryl Zanuck decided he'd had enough of self-sacrifice and would be moving on—Lord began to write a script he called "Forgotten Man." He had a collaborator on the job, Wilson Mizner. Mizner was twenty-four years older than Lord, and a character. With his brother Addison he had been a font of creative ideas, a wit, a writer, and co-owner of the Brown Derby restaurant in Los Angeles. (The Mizners are the subject of a Stephen Sondheim musical, variously known as *Wise Guys* or *Gold*.) Jack Warner was especially fond of Mizner and his jokes. One day, when they were dining at the Brown Derby, the table legs were uneven. "How can you expect anything in Hollywood to be on the level?" quipped Mizner.[1]

Lord and Mizner wrote a script for "Forgotten Man," and then Mizner died on April 3, 1933. But the script went ahead as *Heroes for Sale*, to be directed by William Wellman two years after *The Public Enemy*.[2] *Heroes* was seventy-six minutes, and here is a compressed version of how much Lord and Mizner got into that time. Tom (Richard Barthelmess) is a soldier in the Great War. He is wounded after heroic action and captured by Germans. They give him morphine for his pain, and Tom becomes an addict. When he gets home he discovers that his best pal has taken credit for Tom's heroism. He soldiers on, with time in an asylum, and then unemployment. He gets a job in a laundry, he meets a woman (Loretta Young); he promotes a radical new way of doing laundry—this is a down-to-earth movie. But there is a labor dispute. His woman is killed. And Tom ends up in prison.

This pilgrim's progress is merciless, but when he is set free Tom tries again, and now we are at the time of Franklin Roosevelt's election. Up there on the screen, Tom quotes FDR's inaugural and tells the other characters—and us—that all they have to do is try again and believe. *Heroes for Sale* is still not as well known as it should be, so see it and recognize the bold marriage of pessimism and hope, and see how easily a Warners picture stood up for propaganda—as Tom says, "It takes more than one sock on the jaw to lick a hundred and twenty million people."

Play that picture with *I Am a Fugitive from a Chain Gang*, and the double bill reminds us of Warner Bros' reputation as the most socially conscious or leftist studio outside the Soviet Union. How secure is that reputation, and where did it come from? Darryl Zanuck, as he left Warners, on his way to leadership of the new Twentieth Century–Fox studio, where he would reign for thirty years and make a fortune, claimed he had had a hand in the script for *Heroes for Sale*. And I'm sure he had approved it, and encouraged Lord and Mizner. Zanuck was a boss subject to fits of conscience: at Fox he would be a stalwart defender of John Ford's *The Grapes of Wrath*, as well as Alice Faye musicals. Why not? He had learned at Warners that you had to balance the hard and the soft.

There were also people at the studio who did the actual work, like Robert Lord and William Wellman, like Joan Blondell and Richard Barthelmess, who wanted to believe in their material. Barthelmess had been a big star in the silent era, a classical hero who helped found Inspiration Pictures, and he became a very good actor—you can see that in *Heroes for Sale* and *Only Angels Have Wings*. But he lost his status and at the age of forty-six he gave up acting to enter the naval reserve. He faded away.

Or is that just the film fan slipping into the scenario of legend? It is fascinating to trace the history of social and political responsibility at Warners, in the era that went from Depression to war. In many respects, this is an honorable story that goes above and beyond the record of other studios. But Warners could also be mean-spirited, hypocritical, and eager to make a buck on patriotism. For Jack Warner himself, the war was an opportunity to become an honorary colonel and wear a uniform at the studio.

Warners made plenty of froth and nonsense in the thirties, like anyone else. It indulged in the costume romance of *Anthony Adverse* and *Jezebel;* it did all the Torchy Blane B pictures with Glenda Farrell as the spunky reporter; it played the gangster picture through the decade for fantasy violence and macho posturing. But there was often an undertone in those films that said, look, *this* is what becomes of poor people in our cities.

And Warners made *Black Legion* (1937). This started as a story by Robert Lord, who would also produce the picture, though the script was credited to Abem Finkel and William Wister Haines. It was prompted by a real outrage in Detroit when a WPA administrator was kidnapped and murdered by a fascist, racist organization claiming to be vigilantes. Lord's story offered Frank Taylor, as an ordinary, none-too-intelligent factory worker who is passed over for promotion in favor of "a foreigner," a Pole. In resentment, he joins the Black Legion (a Ku Klux Klan outfit in black robes). He becomes a racist activist in a story that exposes the Legion and ends in Taylor informing on others as he goes off to prison. The role of Taylor was taken by Humphrey Bogart, who had just had a breakthrough playing the vicious gangster Duke Mantee in *The Petrified Forest* (1936). At that time, Bogart was steadily cast as a villain, and there was a grim side to his screen personality well suited to Taylor, a guy without redeeming features. As directed by Archie Mayo, *Black Legion* is an earnest, unrelenting picture, more valuable for its admission about certain realities in America than as drama, or entertainment. Lord was nominated for his story and the film was acclaimed by the National Board of Review, but it did not do well at the box office. It may not have helped that Warners used this selling line: "There's no Paul Muni in *Black Legion*, but there's Humphrey Bogart."[3]

The following year Jack Warner took a special interest in *They Won't Forget*, written by Robert Rossen and Aben Kandel, directed and produced by Mervyn LeRoy. In an unnamed southern town, a teacher is accused of killing a pretty female student (the debut of Lana Turner, aged sixteen). A trial follows, led by a flamboyant and conniving district attorney (played by Claude Rains). The teacher is convicted (wrongly), but the state governor commutes the death sentence, whereupon the teacher is dragged out of jail by a mob and lynched. This was based on a real case (the Leo Frank–Mary Phagan story from 1913), though the film is a freewheeling melodrama. But once again, the awareness of real life in America comes through, and nothing other than the essential movie audience is being indicted. We can always tell ourselves that the real target of the lesson is "other people," and no one knows how to measure the reforming effect of such works. But in many respects, large and small, Hollywood could guide the way people were thinking, and what they were noticing about themselves.

In the late thirties, Warners began to make a number of films that were not ostensibly about the developing crisis in Europe, but which deserve to be interpreted in that light. So it's intriguing to wonder, were they brave, or business as usual?

Paul Muni was regarded as a "great actor," and he was under contract at Warners.[4] His deal allowed him to veto pictures that didn't impress him, without incurring suspensions or penalties. As a consequence, Muni was inclined to prolong his own deliberations and doubts in a way that irritated Jack Warner. More than that, Muni liked to have his wife give comments on the rushes on his own pictures. But uneasiness over Muni had been averted when he was cast in *The Story of Louis Pasteur* (1936), a serious if not solemn celebratory biopic, directed by

William Dieterle and produced by Henry Blanke, another of the good supervisors at Warners. The nobility of Pasteur, and the value of his work, could not be questioned. Muni took the role carefully and slowly, and he won the acting Oscar for it.

The studio drew confidence from this and launched into *The Life of Emile Zola* (1937), directed and produced by the same team. This time, the movie won the Oscar for Best Picture—the first time Warners had had such a victory. The picture had not taken great pains over historical accuracy. Hal Wallis had urged the makeup department to let Muni look like Muni, and not Zola—for no one knew or cared what Emile looked like. As it was made, the film was a Muni vehicle, and its success helped confirm the actor's own opinion of how conscientious and sincere he was. In fact, it drags now and seems burdened with an excessively pious respect for History and its Great Men.

The treatment of Zola's life didn't spend too much time on his literary process. Instead, it fixed on the Dreyfus case, with which Zola was surely identified—he wrote the "J'Accuse" letter against the antisemitic conspiracy that had victimized Captain Alfred Dreyfus (well played by Joseph Schildkraut, who won the Supporting Actor Oscar). The feeling has grown over the decades that the picture was a tacit attack on Hitler and Nazism. But contemporary reviews did not seem to notice that. The *New York Times* said it was "rich, dignified, honest and strong," which is not exactly the language of excitement or urgency.[5] Nor did Warners blur or distract from the esteem in which the film was held—and esteem is seldom close to troublemaking.

But so much history is established in hindsight. Writing long after the war, Jack Warner related that in the mid-thirties he and his wife had been in Europe and had learned that Warners' representative in Berlin, "Joe Kauffman," had been murdered by Nazis in Berlin. "Like many another outnumbered Jew," wrote Jack, "he was trapped in an alley. They hit him with fists and clubs, and kicked the life out of him with their boots, and left him lying there."[6]

It sounds a grisly scene, such as Jack might have put in one of his own pictures. But in fact, as historian Ben Urwand has established, "Joe" was actually "Phil." He was attacked, in 1934, but he survived and left Germany to live in Sweden. Yet Warner made the claim that this murder had prompted him to close down the company office in Berlin.[7] In truth that action had been taken by the German government, in 1934, when it decided that Warner Bros was unsympathetic and a likely source of trouble. Warners still did business in Germany: it was reluctant to lose any foreign market. Moreover, the German consul in Los Angeles, Georg Gyssling, regularly urged Hollywood studios to be considerate of German feelings. When *The Life of Emile Zola* was still in the script stage, Gyssling called the studio and was so insistent that Jack Warner himself cut any line in the film that referred to Dreyfus as a Jew.

Then critical ennobling overtook some of the Errol Flynn pictures. Born in Tasmania in 1909, Flynn had made an amateur film about the voyage of the *Bounty*. He had then gone to England and done a few things on stage, as well as a movie. Warners heard about him, offered him $125 a week, and shipped him to the United States. Against an early wish to use Robert Donat, the studio tried Flynn as *Captain Blood* (1935). It turned out the camera loved him: his deal rose to $750 a week. Then add a mustache?

What followed testified to the whole theory of stars. As Jack put it, "I knew we had grabbed the brass ring in our thousand-to-one shot spin with Flynn. When you see a meteor stab in the sky, or a bomb explode, or a fire sweep across a dry hillside, the picture is vivid and remains alive in your mind. So it was with Errol Flynn."[8] A few years later, Jack was ready to retire that meteor because Flynn was so often drunk on set, and in the habit of alienating his best directors. Hal Wallis decided that Flynn had little interest in filmmaking and often forgot his lines.

For a while, however, the actor was handsome, well spoken, breezy, athletic, fine-tuned to romance, and simply likable. In considering Flynn, one realizes how many Warners actors had an edge of darkness, a brooding quality that made their spirits seem higher. That is how Flynn and Olivia de Havilland were such a tonic together. Flynn was at his best in costume, preferably with long hair and a rapier in his hand. He needed unequivocal enemies—scoundrels of the seas, the French, the Spanish, the Turks, the Sioux, or even the Sheriff of Nottingham. By the early forties, he was at $7,000 a week.

He had a constancy on screen that women in his life despaired of. But that's fair enough: in the 1930s, people wanted actors to save their dull souls. *The Adventures of Robin Hood* is a burnished adventure romance for boys and girls, graced with color, an exhilarating score by Erich Wolfgang Korngold, and a parade of supporting actors such as Warners commanded: Claude Rains as Prince John, Basil Rathbone as Sir Guy of Gisbourne, Eugene Pallette as Friar Tuck, Alan Hale as Little John, Una O'Connor as Marian's maid. But is that film really a warning against tyranny and a plea for the socialist paradise of those merry men in the forest? I don't think Jack Warner or his people were in the habit of seeing the allegory in their films. (If you did, Sherwood might have looked gay.) They trusted the immediate story, and putting it across so that the sophistication of 1938 technology prettified the legend of England in the fourteenth century. Sherwood was in Chico.

The Sea Hawk came later, in July 1940, when much of the world was at war already. This one is in black and white, directed by Michael Curtiz on a budget of $1.7 million—expensive for then and a measure of the film's spectacle. Howard Koch wrote it with Seton Miller, and Koch would later be blacklisted for Communist associations. But is this story of an English privateer (a Drake-like hero) seeking to harass the assembling Armada really a fable about the threat of fascism? Are Don Álvarez (Claude Rains) and Philip of Spain (Montagu Love) meant to be Hitler figures? Or was the film preoccupied with trying to get Henry Daniell to fence without falling over in the duel scene, while wondering why Flynn was late on set day after day and often so fatigued? It did have Flora Robson as Queen Elizabeth I delivering a speech intended to inspire the English audience (and clearly influenced by the 1937 British film *Fire over England*). It had Korngold again, and it seems like a picture made six thousand miles and many levels of consciousness away from the experience of war.

You can't expect allegory or subtlety in a film to be called *Confessions of a Nazi Spy*, and that's what Warners opened in May 1939.[9] This venture was actively promoted by Harry Warner, and it reflects his earnestness. It was directed by Anatole Litvak, with a script by Milton Krims and John Wexley; and it was produced by the reliable Robert Lord. Krims was sent to New York in disguise to infiltrate Bund meetings. The project was then kept secret as *Storm over America*. Wexley loved the collaborative mood at Warners among writers and producers, though he said Hal Wallis was "a cold icicle, impenetrable," while Jack Warner was often "a clown."[10]

Confessions was based on the memoir of the former FBI officer who had been responsible for uncovering a Nazi plot in America. Warners moved on this project, ahead of any other studio, but it was at pains to be accurate with it. So the story is an espionage thriller in which a determined FBI man (Edward G. Robinson) uncovers an extensive plot that involves Nazis played by Francis Lederer, George Sanders, and several German actors who had recently fled to America.

The German government was offended. Members of the Bund tried to sue Warners and break up screenings. But the *New*

York Times film critic Frank Nugent went to the heart of the matter: "Hitler won't like it; neither will Goebbels. Frankly, we were not too favorably impressed either."[11] It's not very good, which always tends to compromise courage and relevance. In 1940, the biopic tendency came back with Robinson in *Dr. Ehrlich's Magic Bullet*, about the man who had found a cure for syphilis—though Warners chose Ehrlich more because he was German and Jewish than because of the malady he targeted.

Robinson then opened in *The Sea Wolf* in the spring of 1941, a parable of Nazi tyranny—if you were inclined to read it that way. Wolf Larson commands a ship by dint of cruel power and an intimidated crew. The story came from Jack London, for a sea adventure staged in the studio tank, and a film noir with a jaundiced view of male togetherness. Robinson's Larson is unsure whether he loathes mankind or himself the more. There are expert supporting performances from John Garfield, Alexander Knox, Barry Fitzgerald, and Gene Raymond, and Ida Lupino does one of her nasty waifs, with mist and sea salt hanging on her lips. Who directed it? Michael Curtiz—again— and he hardly puts a foot wrong. But the mix of gloomy adventure and political undertones is something no other studio would have attempted.

Warners' official war films would talk about courage, but they don't always achieve the right level of fearful experience. *Sergeant York* was a very big picture for Warners, with Gary Cooper playing Alvin York, the hero from the Great War (done with York's blessing). It opened in September 1941 and earned $16 million on a budget of $1.4 million. As a Howard Hawks film, it ought to be sharp and wry, but it's so much more ponderous and complacent than *To Have and Have Not*, which only flirts with combat and war—but flirtation was Hawks's abiding subject.

There were people at Warners who had an understanding of what was going on in Europe in the late thirties, and what the war was about. They more or less shared hopes for social reform and liberal enlightenment, and they were able to push some of that into their pictures. In time, that effort would be foolishly rebuked for being pro-Communist, no matter that during the war the Soviet Union had been an official ally.

In that brief season, the government prevailed upon Warners to make a film called *Mission to Moscow*, about the American ambassador to the Soviet Union, Joseph E. Davies. (The company had prospered with ambassadors in the past.) Jack said FDR pressured him personally to do this picture. Michael Curtiz directed and Howard Koch wrote it—against his instinct that it was going to be dull. The film uses a lot of Soviet newsreel; it presents Stalin as an admirable character; but it has little story, and it asks Walter Huston, as Davies, to move through various tableaux as if they were back projections. But Davies's book had been a best-seller, and the film did well enough because for that moment Americans wanted to think well of their Soviet brothers. It opened in May 1943, and took more than two hours to express its uncertain sense of occasion. The film protests its own truthfulness, but the critic Manny Farber was alert to the problem: "We didn't deserve that Mr. Davies should have met the Warner Brothers."[12]

By 1947, this climate had changed. Jack Warner testified to the House Un-American Activities Committee. He said *Mission to Moscow* had been made in a bad moment, not for posterity— as if any picture had any other impulse. He said he was aghast at the menace of reds in the picture business, and was pleased to name them. But in his cross-examination by Robert Stripling, he gave away other truths. Stripling was eager to get Jack to admit that *Mission to Moscow* was a pack of lies and half-truths designed as propaganda. This was a fair estimate of the picture, but Jack was shy about admitting that Warners might have been taken advantage of and made a boring movie. So Stripling put it to him, "Well, do you suppose that your picture influenced the people who saw it in this country, the millions of people who saw it in this country?"[13] In other words, what did movies actually do to people?

Jack considered a moment and said what was expected of any mogul in the picture business, then or now: "In my opinion, I can't see how it would influence anyone. We were in war and when you are in a fight you don't ask who the fellow is who is helping you."[14]

This wisdom did not sink in too far. Howard Koch and many others were victimized for having shared in socialist sentiments. Warners was always better at seeing the place for courage in domestic situations, and as a female characteristic.

So I'd like to urge an unlikely candidate in this chapter, *The Hard Way*, also made for 1943. It's the story of two sisters, played by Ida Lupino and Joan Leslie, in which the older one uses the younger one not just to make a living but to have an emotional life for herself. Directed by Vincent Sherman, produced by Jerry Wald, it was written by two distinguished writers—Daniel Fuchs and Peter Viertel. It took bravery for Ida Lupino to play an unpleasant, manipulative woman, often without makeup. She was as scared as any beautiful actress fearful of risking her gold. But it turned out the best film she ever made and one of the finest Warner pictures about bitter truths in ordinary life.[15]

Lasting value was more likely there than in anything as epic or boastful as *Objective, Burma!* (1945), a view of Errol Flynn winning that jungle war, so blind to British and Australian efforts that the film had to be withdrawn in Britain for a year. The film also had this bloodthirsty recommendation: "The Japanese should be wiped off the face of the earth."[16]

Since I started this chapter with Robert Lord, let me close by updating his story. A graduate of Harvard, he had been a stalwart at the studio throughout the thirties, urging radical ideas into many stories. Then he went off to war for nearly four years. When he was discharged he wrote to Jack Warner, in

August 1945, and offered himself as production head at the studio—the post that his supporter Hal Wallis had relinquished a year before.

Lord wrote, "I think that I can be instrumental in helping to produce some pictures of high quality and strong box-office appeal. I think I can administer the studio quietly, politely, efficiently and without attempts to become a God, as several of your previous Executive Producers have attempted."[17] He proposed himself on a five-year contract at $250,000 a year, which was not unreasonable, just as the tone of his letter was calm enough to promise a useful appointment.

Maybe calm frightened Jack. He said no thanks, and sent Lord official release forms. But he wanted Lord "to know my brother and I have the very warmest feelings towards you and always will have."[18]

Lord moved on and joined Humphrey Bogart at Santana Productions. By then, Bogie had had his fill of Jack, too. Together he and Lord made a number of films, including *In a Lonely Place*, the masterpiece in Robert Lord's career and a piercing portrait of being alone in Hollywood.

But the steady routine of action and conflict was not everything. Imagine you are at the movies in 1941 waiting for *Sergeant York* or *The Sea Wolf*. Then here comes something else, seven and a half minutes of cartoon, as uninhibited a celebration of the rascal as anything Jimmy Cagney ever dared.

In some dullsville American town, lurid in early Technicolor, there lives a humble man, without kin or company. He has a brown derby hat and a speech impediment. His name is Elmer Fudd and no one knows he is there. But even Fudds think of companionship, and so in the merry month of May he takes a walk; we see his droopy shoes and legs on a sidewalk. He pauses briefly at a sign for a "Lingerie Sale"—does he feel pangs of desire?

He trudges on to Gumbiner's Pet Store. And there in the window is a gray rabbit, priced once at $150.00, but marked down now to 99 cents.

So Fudd acquires "a pet." It's a rabbit, but it looks like a hare, with ears standing up as long and straight as. . . . In the window, this bunny seemed demure, but as Fudd plods home with the box under his arm, the rabbit peeps out and asks, "What you got in that box, Doc?" If only Fudd had known.

The credits of the movie introduced him as "Bugs Bunny." At last Warner Bros had found their guy, with whiskers for a mustache. Bugs is an invader: he eats any and every vegetable he can see; he will take over Chez Fudd and make it his hotel; he is a trickster and a demon, without scruple or shame—but wordy (in seven minutes he comes on with "frankly," "irony," "humiliate," "responsible," and "cad"). And he talks to the camera! He sounds like Groucho Marx as well as Cagney.

Bugs takes over the house, like a commando requisitioning civilian property in a time of crisis—this film opens January 5, 1941 (a day before FDR's Four Freedoms speech). He wants Fudd's bathroom and his bed. He transforms the tranquil Fudd salon, turning on the lights, getting the music going, and leading Elmer in a frantic dance—is this the first gay scene in a Warner Bros film! And if Fudd thinks to complain, Bugs slaps him around (without a grapefruit) and cries out "This means war!" In January 1941, as the rest of the studio is getting ready to be patriotic and brave, here is a whole movie that ridicules war!

It is called *Elmer's Pet Rabbit*, directed by Chuck Jones (Charles Jones in the credits), produced by Leon Schlesinger, and with the voice of Mel Blanc still working out how to play Bugs. This is my passing nod to Warners cartoons and the great men just named—add Friz Freleng, Tex Avery, Bob Clampett, Frank Tashlin, and so many others to the roll of honor, heroes even if Jack wanted to close down the unit from time to time.

And here it is, the mayhem of liberty, the orgy of self and unrestrained id just when Warner Bros and that wabbit Jack were putting their hand on their heart—left side chest, front, idiot, underneath the medals!—and saying, "Oh, no more gangster pictures for us. We're at war!"[19]

Humphrey Bogart and Lauren Bacall in *The Big Sleep*—sooner or later, a man and a woman have to talk

15

Bogart

IT WAS A PRINCIPLE of stardom that actors stayed the same, film after film, decade after decade. Bugs never aged, or grew up. The process established a brand, an appearance, an attitude, made sure the public liked it, and then repeated it for as long as possible. Of course, the actors and actresses grew older, though some did anything they could manage to delay that or hide it. Nearly twenty years after he had begun, in 1949, Warners persuaded Jimmy Cagney to be a gangster again. He had mixed feelings—he was so much gentler a guy in reality. And he was older, bulkier, less cocksure. Those differences added to the pathos of his Cody Jarrett in *White Heat*. But Warners was clinging to the past and assuring us it was the old Jim. Decades later, Jimmy Cagney is the montage of all his bustling, dancing hoods. In 1975, Philippe Mora made a documentary like that, *Brother Can You Spare a Dime?*, which is the 1930s as seen in Cagney pictures.

But one star did change, and the shift meant more than just lifting Humphrey Bogart's horizons. It was a significant alteration in the idea of what a man should be. It is also close to the heart of the Warner Brothers dream in which an outlaw might become a sultry paragon.

Humphrey DeForest Bogart was born in New York City on Christmas Day, 1899, the son of a surgeon and a magazine illustrator.[1] Of all the actors raised in the Warners gangster tradition, Bogart was the best born, from the most affluent family. He went to Trinity and Phillips Academy, and he was apparently headed for Yale. But he was unruly and averse to his own advantages, so he joined the navy instead as a seaman. Louise Brooks knew him as a young man, and she saw a gentleman anxious to hide his privilege beneath a rough act.[2] For several generations, the movies were the natural testing ground for young men who wondered whether they were brave, afraid, or just a regular mix of those moods.

Humphrey set out to be an actor, and a young male lead in polite stage plays. But he was not beautiful or energetic and not quite relaxed; his voice had a bit of a lisp and a rasp. He got some good notices but he didn't catch on. He tried Hollywood once sound had arrived, but again he made little impact in the years when Cagney and Robinson were thriving. It was only in 1935 that he had a personal success on Broadway in Robert Sherwood's play *The Petrified Forest*. When Warners decided to film it, his costar Leslie Howard told the studio it had to retain Bogart as Duke Mantee (Warners had been thinking of Edward G. Robinson—it was usually thinking of someone else). Bogart is extravagantly nasty in that part—in truth, he's overdone. But the film did well so Warners gave him a six-month contract as a villain-type in its diet of crime pictures.

He made more than twenty films in the next few years, on supporting-part money. There were a few worthwhile jobs: the district attorney in *Marked Woman*, the bigot in *Black Legion*.

But as a rule he was a hoodlum who ended badly, who snarled and whimpered, and often took a bullet from someone like Cagney. That's how he ended up in *Angels with Dirty Faces* and *The Roaring Twenties*. The actor was depressed with himself. He had two failed marriages; he drank too much; and he had a bitter, needling personality that made enemies. Some people find him interesting as the Irish groom with Bette Davis in *Dark Victory*—others think he's uneasy in the role. He had married for a third time—three actresses—but this wife, Mayo Methot, was a worse drunk than he was. They fought in public. He was losing his hair. He was forty and making about $1,000 a week. Nothing was happening. Bogart was typecast as a dirty rat, but not a king rat, and he was hurt. He had no ease, and stars need to like themselves. One secret to being Jack Warner was that he knew he was a terrific guy.

W. R. Burnett, the author of *Little Caesar*, was still writing. In 1940, he published a new novel, *High Sierra*. This is how it began:

> Early in the twentieth century, when Roy Earle was a happy boy on an Indiana farm, he had no idea that at thirty-seven he'd be a pardoned ex-convict driving alone through the Nevada-California desert towards an ambiguous destiny in the Far West.[3]

John Huston read the book and wrote straightaway to Hal Wallis: "It would be very easy for this to be made into the conventional gangster picture, which is exactly what it should not be."[4] Huston had sensed that Earle could be a tragic figure, or a tough guy with an inner life. This was an early instinct (and it was homing in on the fellow Huston hoped he was), but it was prescient. War doesn't actually want unbridled gangsters, or unreservedly violent men. The real test on courage and self-respect is more complex—a good soldier has to seem thoughtful, reluctant, and even fatalistic. He can be an infantry private, but he needs a bit of the captain, too, the phlegmatic officer type. Huston was hired to do a script for *High Sierra*, and he saw Earle as a veteran weary of "conventional gangster attitudes." This was a man who wanted to "break out" of his hoodlum existence.

Warners liked the project and saw it as ideal for Paul Muni. But Muni had fought with Huston on *Juarez*, and now he pulled out of doing Roy Earle. At which point, Warners fired the great actor! Maybe this was all a setup to get rid of an expensive egotist. The part then failed to win George Raft, Robinson, or Cagney. Bogart was the fallback casting, probably with encouragement from Huston. But as the picture was set up, Ida Lupino (the female lead) got bigger billing than Bogart. The studio was enthusiastic about her because of her witness-stand mad scene in *They Drive by Night* (in which Bogart had been second male lead to Raft).[5]

Earle fails in *High Sierra:* his hope for finding a sweetheart collapses; renewed criminal life turns out disastrous. He is shot down in the Sierra peaks. But he is a winning character. His hair is going gray. He is tired and disillusioned, but he has respect for others. The film was good enough to start a change in the public's view of Bogart. Then allow that it helped improve his sense of himself. There he was up on screen, halfway decent, an admirable loner and with chemistry between him and the Lupino part (Mayo Methot was jealous enough to hang around the set). This was the first time on screen that Bogart had played a man who might deserve a love scene.

Just as important was his growing bond with Huston. Warners was impressed with Huston's writing, and with the sheer presence of the man (John would be an actor too), so they offered him a chance to direct. With characteristic nerve, Huston opted for a property the studio had already failed with twice, Dashiell Hammett's *The Maltese Falcon*. Considering how many gangster films Warners had done, it's odd that the studio had not succeeded with a type we now take for granted, the private eye, in this case Sam Spade.

Here was an even better example of the reformed tough guy: laconic, sarcastic, capable of violence, but working on the side of justice, or whatever it was that might oppose Sydney Greenstreet, Peter Lorre, and Mary Astor in their pursuit of the stuff dreams are made of, the Falcon. Huston's Spade is more emphatic and cruel than Hammett's. Huston had appreciated that needling aspect of Bogart's personality and seen a way to use it. Nearly everyone in the picture was getting a break: it was Huston's debut, Greenstreet's first film, a breakthrough for Lorre, a new chance for Mary Astor, and it placed Bogart as a droll, goading ringmaster. Put it next to something like *Each Dawn I Die* (1939) and it seems so modern. Kissing Astor but then slapping her, bantering with Greenstreet, teasing Lorre— Spade was said to be in a tight spot, but Bogart was relaxed.

Shot fast, for less than $400,000, *The Maltese Falcon* opened in October 1941, and it was a big success. After a full decade, the studio began to understand what it had as a property—but Bogart was getting the message, too. Jack Warner was so excited by the result that he wondered whether Hammett could be persuaded to write a sequel with the same characters. He never did, but they have stayed in our heads. Greenstreet and Lorre would be partnered at Warners in nine films. It was an instance of the culture of supporting players rising like cream, and it was a strength of the Warner stock company.

By December 1941, people at Warners were looking at a treatment for a never-produced play, *Everybody Comes to Rick's*, and several were thinking it might suit the new Bogart. There was second-guessing on all the casting, but Bogart was always the favorite, even if hardly anyone noted that the actor had never done a serious love scene on film before, or even been in love. But of course America had not been in the new war before, and somehow *Casablanca* was going to have to marry those two large motifs. By February 1942, Hal Wallis was thinking Bogart and Ann Sheridan, as yet unaware that Ilsa had to be foreign in what was going to be a nearly screwball league-of-nations movie—all shot in Burbank.

Not the least virtue of *Casablanca* is that Rick likes nearly everyone: he cherishes Sam; he's prepared to stroll off into a misty future with Louis; he respects Greenstreet's Ferrari; he relies on Dalio's croupier; he is happy with his team of employees. Granted his resolute isolation or neutrality and his man-of-the-world apartness, still he is a kind of tuxedo Robin Hood. Yes, he adores Ilsa and would do something crazy for her—and Bogart does show the wounds left after their broken affair. But he admires Victor, too. He may have to kill Strasser, but Rick has something like Hemingway's respect for a dangerous lion in the veldt.

By the time *Casablanca* opened (November 1942), Americans were at war, dying, or separated from loved ones. So remind yourself what an adroit masquerade it was, and how far a fantasy of authority, courage, and romantic altruism catered to anxious men and women in war. Imagine that Rick might have had a mistress, living at his place, and you can see how much untidier the film would have been. But tidiness is its charm. That's in Curtiz's camera style, and the flawless cast, and in fate, too. The film had bizarre good fortune: it opened just as the Allies took the real city of Casablanca. Did Jack Warner sometimes wonder whether he had arranged that? He *was* a colonel by then.

Casablanca was the second Warners picture to win the Best Picture Oscar. Bogart was nominated as Best Actor for the first time. The picture cost just under $900,000, and it earned $3.7 million on its first release. It keeps on earning. So it's worth stressing that Bogart did it for $2,200 a week, which was less than half the pay level of several other Warner stars. *Casablanca* made him—as everyone knew—but he had let the project work for the studio, and he never earned a residual check on the film.

Warners learned from the picture, including the appeal of a café where a gang of stylish outsiders mingled. Hemingway's *To Have and Have Not* (published in 1937) could easily be a café film—with intriguing upstairs rooms. Marcel Dalio would go from being croupier at Rick's Café Américain to "Frenchie," in charge of a similar place in Martinique. It was also a variation on the *Casablanca* motif of a detached figure joining the great cause, so Harry Morgan the private operator agrees to assist the Free French against the forces of Vichy. But that's taking the film more gravely than it really requires. You can cite *To Have and Have Not* as a war film if you like, but don't neglect its fascination with knowing how to whistle, leaning in doorways, innuendo, snide flirt, and a new kind of outrageous girl. It's not that Howard Hawks ignored war—he had made *Sergeant York* and *Air Force* at Warners—but he was best left to his own dreams and devices. And he recognized in Bogart an appealing, dry insolence that needed only one extra—a girl who was more insolent.

Lauren Bacall (as she would become) was the most striking young Warners discovery until James Dean.[6] There was something else about her that was unusual: Betty Joan Perske, born in 1924 in the Bronx, was Jewish and "panic-stricken" that her discoverer, Howard Hawks, would realize that.[7] Hawks's wife, Slim, had seen her on the cover of *Harper's Bazaar* and suggested the girl to her husband.[8] That was playing with fire for a wife, and one neglected irony of the film is that Hawks was surely bent on seducing Bacall until she and Bogart fell in love. Bogart was still married to Mayo Methot and hounded by her jealousy. His thing with Bacall—or Slim, as the film called her— might have been heavenly for anyone who loved movie romance, but it was hellish and awkward in real life. The players must have been grateful to have their movie dialogue to fall back on, supplied by Jules Furthman and William Faulkner. And Hawks may have had his brief way with Bacall—she was under a personal service contract to him.

The film is the story of a nineteen-year-old who seems to have the experience of a mature Carole Lombard or Marlene Dietrich, and who finds herself adrift in Martinique and inclined to wonder whether Harry Morgan has a light, any interest in learning how to whistle, and an invitation to engage in crosstalk. Is she an outrageous hooker, or a hook to catch our eye and ear? Hawks made films about men and women looking at one another and sparring with words, kisses, and the larger suggestion that there was no need to abide by censorship. Bacall's character—hardly named, but it's Marie—is independent, tricky, and sure to answer Harry back, yet she's utterly malleable in yielding to his dream. She's the perfect teenage sexpot for a man more than twice her age who wants to think he's a loner and she's a lucky find. It's his fantasy, as shameless as it is irresistible. It's *Lolita* without a breath of guilt.

It's also the first film considered in this book that, while made at Warners, is defiantly private or personal or the work of a director as single-minded as, say, Bonnard painting breakfast tables or his wife in the bath, no matter what else might be going on in the real world. For Hawks there is no real world, there is just the dream.[9] The public discovery that this provocateuse and her tickled father were in love, and surely in sex, was one of the best gifts to publicity in Hollywood history. So Bogart had more reasons to feel happy, or even smug; that may inspire the serenity with which he walks through the picture. It's strange now to look back on this exquisite film and realize there really was a war going on. Warner Bros made the movie and paid for it, opened it and prospered on it. But the film is above and beyond that context. It's like a great (yet phantom) Gothic cathedral, still standing, but oblivious of the culture in which people once believed in its God. It is a masterpiece—and that's reason to take note: while Warner Brothers was happy to make very good, entertaining films, it had not the least interest in masterpieces. For all the studio knew, there could and should have been a proviso in the Production Code against master-pieces, for if word ever got out that they were possible, the whole scam might be over.

And if you want any more insolence, just to rub it in, the team did it again, and did it even better in *The Big Sleep*. Some commentators reckon that the originator of that alleged story, Raymond Chandler, believed the big sleep was death. But that's too solemn or sentimental for Hawks. The sleep is there to fur-nish the dream, and its rapture sweeps aside story.

Still, it is a film taken from Chandler's 1939 novel in which a private detective makes gestures towards solving "a case." Several people are stylishly killed—the death of Harry Jones (Elisha Cook) is still one of the best murders on screen. You can call it a film noir because of those events, the detective and his doll, and the low-key allure of the lighting. But you can as easily label it a screwball comedy because its life and rhythm are in a couple talking at cross purposes or like lovers doodling while they're doing sex talk on the phone. It does not matter whether Bogart and Bacall were happy together in life (I hope they had their moments), because they have 114 minutes of splendor in this film.

It should go on forever. The idea that the mystery needs to be settled is specious. The external reality of Los Angeles is a joke because the film dwells on and worships its sets, even if one sometimes claims to be a street in the city or a lane in the hills. Who would not listen to General Sternwood (Charles Waldron) reminiscing about his ingeniously wicked daughters? Surely his butler, Norris, has stories we might coax out of him. Don't we deserve detail from that sourpuss Agnes (Sonia Dar-rin) on scenarios about the rotten time life gives her? And I have not even come to Dorothy Malone and Martha Vickers yet, treasures who make do with a few sly minutes when they merit hours and days.

It's not so much that *The Big Sleep* is an exceptional picture. It's rather more that an ecstatic state of pure and daft movie has been achieved, and it stretches out like a desert or an ocean. In its entire history, Hollywood got to this prospect only a very few times—a dozen seems generous—and two of those films were made, back to back, at Warner Brothers.

16

After the War, Before the End

As WAR ENDED, Warner Bros was exuberant. It was pleased to think the crisis was over; it was eager to regain its European market as quickly as possible; and it was excited at the idea of reunited families ready to go to the movies. So it proved: in 1946 and 1947, the studio reported its biggest profits ever—$19 million and $22 million. For a moment it seemed as if Warners could do no wrong. It even rescued Joan Crawford.

Crawford had been all her working life at MGM, as the common woman, the bad girl, the ambitious tramp, who offset the studio's company of ladies (Garbo, Jeanette MacDonald, Norma Shearer, Greer Garson, Margaret Sullavan).[1] She had been there eighteen years and become a national favorite. But her box office was in decline, and the studio was not offering her its best roles. In 1943, never short on courage, Crawford said she would leave, and Metro agreed that her contract should be dropped by mutual consent. She was thirty-nineish, and her "wide, hurt eyes" (Scott Fitzgerald) were more desperate than ever. Fitzgerald said that if Joan had to lie in a movie, "she would practically give a representation of Benedict Arnold selling West Point to the British."[2] Jack Warner jumped in with a new offer of $500,000 for three pictures. There wasn't too much to lose: Crawford was primed for a big challenge—but it had to be the right material, something fit for a star and those rueful eyes.

Warners had bought the rights to the James M. Cain novel *Mildred Pierce*, published in 1941. But one story editor at the studio understood its problem: "As Cain wrote the novel all the characters in it, including Mildred, were unpleasant. It is well known that in a successful motion picture the audience must be able to identify itself with the interests of certain good characters as against certain bad ones. At the same time the immoral activities of Mildred actually were unscreenable because of the Production Code."[3]

Warners had had doubts about a project full of marital breakdown, lousy parent-daughter relations, adulterous sex, and Cain's regular estimate that people were obsessed with money and sex. Bette Davis had declined the part. Then Barbara Stanwyck refused it. There were early troubles in getting a script that the Breen Office would contemplate without fits. But Crawford remained keen to do it: Mildred was her idea of a social upstart becoming a success. Jack gave the project to Jerry Wald, a writer who wanted to produce. Michael Curtiz was lined up to direct, much against his will. And Ranald Mac-Dougall was charged with cleaning up Cain's act. It was Wald who had the idea of telling the story in flashback as a police station confession; it was MacDougall who cut a lot of the sexual wandering. But Curtiz was obstinate. He didn't want to do the picture, and that was rare in a man blessed with chronic versatility—hadn't he done *Robin Hood*, *Casablanca*, and *Yankee Doodle Dandy*, making a hit out of James Cagney's impersonation of George M. Cohan (and helping Cagney get his Oscar)? But on Crawford, he was outspoken: "She comes over here with her high-hat airs and her goddamn shoulder pads! I won't work with her. She's through, washed up."[4]

Then cameraman Ernie Haller worked out a way to photograph Crawford, with a noir shadow line on her forehead, so those eyes felt more needy. And in the event Curtiz made the novelette look like silky trash. There is a more recent version of *Mildred Pierce*, done by Todd Haynes for HBO (2011), with Kate Winslet in the lead. It is far more faithful to Cain, and it works away at social realism, but it misses the melodrama that Curtiz caught so well: the HBO series is 336 minutes; the 1945 *Mildred Pierce* settles for 111. You can still feel the shock over the daughter Veda's treachery (played with glittering spite by Ann Blyth, aged sixteen). The Warners version stretched audience expectations about what was decent, and how an abandoned wife might have to look after herself. There were women alone and broken homes after the war, as well as optimism renewed; and sometimes one became the other over a weekend. *Mildred Pierce* opened two months after Hiroshima. People make fun of Crawford nowadays, but she knew what crisis was and how important the role was. She understood Mildred (she had trouble ahead with her own children). She got the Oscar, and the film earned $5.6 million on a cost of $1.4 million.

Mildred Pierce and *The Big Sleep* contributed to those record profit numbers, and they promised surgent careers for the two stars. Yet it didn't work out that way. Crawford would never have another success like *Mildred Pierce*. Bogart's salary nearly doubled with *Casablanca*, but after *The Big Sleep* he did one flawed picture after another, some of them movies that the ordinary Bogart fan hardly knows: *Conflict, Dead Reckoning, The Two Mrs. Carrolls, Dark Passage, Key Largo.* Louise Brooks said that the tough guy was too accustomed to doing as he was told. *Key Largo* and *Dark Passage* were with Bacall again, and they have better reputations. But the second is contrived, once you get over the gimmick of Bogart being the camera, and *Key Largo* (despite the direction of John Huston) is a talky piece of soul-searching where Bogart and Bacall are overshadowed by Edward G. Robinson doing his most deliciously odious gangster, Johnny Rocco, sweating in his bath, snarling past his cigar and whispering obscene promises in Bacall's ear, and by Claire Trevor, who is outstanding as Rocco's aging mistress.

But as Bogart faltered after *The Big Sleep*, and chose or accepted dubious roles, so Bacall—a sensation in her debut—quickly became a difficult actress to cast and someone who seemed to have lost her appeal. At twenty-five, she didn't look like the public idea of her. Or did she ever understand it? That teenage wanton that Hawks noticed was impossible in other eyes, including her own. To see her in *Young Man with a Horn* (1950, another Michael Curtiz picture), playing an acidic, self-destructive, probably lesbian "intellectual," is to marvel that anyone let her take the role. It also throws welcome attention on the other woman in that film, the vibrantly fresh Doris Day, a buttercup who might be the child of Joan Blondell.[5]

For the best part of ten years, Doris Day had been a band singer, with Les Brown. She did plenty of radio, and she had a hit with "Embraceable You," which spoke to every wartime relationship undergoing separation. She was singing at a party in Los Angeles when the idea arose that she might step in for a pregnant Betty Hutton in *Romance on the High Seas* (1948), where she sang "It's Magic." Warners put Day under contract; she proved their most lucrative signing in the postwar years and a way back to musicals for the studio. For the most part these were smotheringly cheerful, lightweight get-togethers that failed to use Day's sturdy personality. The titles tell the story: *My Dream Is Yours, It's a Great Feeling, Tea for Two, I'll See You in My Dreams, By the Light of the Silvery Moon, On Moonlight Bay, Lucky Me.* Gordon MacRae and Gene Nelson were her regular partners; there were sweet, cheery songs; and Doris was encouraged to make decent fun of the proceedings—without ever revealing that she could be funny or sexy.

The films made money; the public cherished Day. But two of them deserve special attention. *Calamity Jane* (1953) was Jack Warner's attempt to rip off *Annie Get Your Gun* with the invention of a tomboy singing heroine out West. But one of its songs, the lush "Secret Love," by Sammy Fain and Paul Francis Webster, was a big success, and it would be taken up by the gay community as an anthem. Doris was not gay—indeed, she had a track record with disastrous men. But she is spunky and bold as Calamity. The next year, she did *Young at Heart*, with a melancholy Frank Sinatra. This is a drama in which he is a depressed songwriter who drifts into a household of women (it includes Dorothy Malone and Ethel Barrymore). There is a suicidal edge to the story, and Doris rose to it. One longs for more films with her and Sinatra as a team, just as she must have wished that Warners would trust her as an actress.

But here was the studio once tied to male stars and manly attitudes, trying to promote Bacall, Crawford, and Doris Day—and Jane Wyman. In 1946, Jerry Wald was doing all he could to persuade the studio to do *Johnny Belinda*, the rural Canadian story of a deaf-mute girl who is raped. This plight called out for the wide-eyed apprehension of Jane Wyman. Wald could see the picture—like a perfect holdup. He wrote to Steve Trilling in the front office:

> You know, frankly, what I should do is take the notes I wrote you on *Mildred Pierce* and just substitute *Johnny Belinda*, because they all run down the same road, primitive stories told in a slick, new fashion. When are you going to get wise to the fact that you can tell a corny story, with basic values, in a very slick, dressed-up fashion. When you tell a corny story in a corny fashion, you end up with junk. Certainly there is no cornier story than *Humoresque*. Let's face it. But it is so

slickly mounted that you forget this is the tired, old mother-love story and find, as a substitute a triangle story with a mother, son and married woman.[6]

Humoresque was the next Crawford vehicle, in which Joan played a society woman involved with a brilliant, headstrong violinist (played by John Garfield, but with Isaac Stern's hands on the strings). This was written by Clifford Odets, with some scorn, and audiences found it far-fetched and overheated. Producing it, Wald had tried to keep Crawford's image ordinary—he wanted plainer clothes and fewer boxed shoulders—then somehow Joan's eyes just made the shoulders grow. But *Johnny Belinda* worked: that slickness turned out as greased pathos, and it won an Oscar for Wyman, impetus that would help her end her marriage to Ronald Reagan, a supporting player at Warners whose career seemed to be trailing away. Wyman was past thirty, playing a far younger girl, but the novelty of her ordeal carried the day. So twice in four years, with Joan and Jane, Warners had carried off the Best Actress Oscar.

The new openness to women at Warners was still a guys' game. And some guys did hanker after old habits. Gangster films had been put on hold during the war lest they give a misleading impression of the home of the brave while sacrifices were being made. But there were stirrings. Two young writers, Ben Roberts and Ivan Goff, were given a brief treatment (by Virginia Kellogg) and told to come up with a gangster story. They went away, thought, and came back to the effective head of production, Steve Trilling: "We'd like to do Ma Barker and have the gangster with a mother complex and play it against Freudian implications that she's driving him to do these things, and he's driving himself to self-destruction. Play it like a Greek tragedy. They said, 'Fellas . . . ?' We said, 'Believe us, it will work. And there's only one man who can play this and make the rafters rock. That is Jimmy Cagney.'"[7]

This presented a problem. Cagney had walked away from Warners after *Yankee Doodle Dandy* and vowed never to return. Jack Warner didn't want him back. The two men were fixed in loathing. But Cagney's independent career had had its setbacks: he had lost a lot of money adapting William Saroyan for *The Time of Your Life.* So he agreed to play Cody Jarrett in *White Heat:* it was the best film he would ever make. This was under the direction of Raoul Walsh, who had joined the studio in the late thirties and done a string of fine pictures: *High Sierra, The Strawberry Blonde* (with Cagney), *Gentleman Jim* (Errol Flynn as boxer Jim Corbett), *Pursued* (a psychological Western, with the young Robert Mitchum).

But *White Heat* relied on its script and the novel idea that a gangster might be mentally disturbed—in a mother-loving way. Jarrett is an older Cagney, a man of innate violence who dreads his debilitating headaches and sometimes curls up on his mother's lap. I suggested earlier that Bette Davis could have played this scene, but that should not detract from the somber compassion that Margaret Wycherly brings to it. The lap scene is still breathtaking, not just unexpected and close to farce, but filled with emotional madness. Since it began, the Warners gangster picture had believed in mothers, but now that came with pathology. You could play *White Heat* with *Psycho* so that each film enriched and explained the other.

White Heat is a gangster picture, with Virginia Mayo and Steve Cochran ably delivering the slut wife and the treacherous associate. But it is also a study in betrayal, with Edmond O'Brien as the undercover agent who infiltrates the Jarrett gang but comes to earn Cody's misplaced fondness. More than any other gangster Cagney played, Cody Jarrett is on the edge of tragedy. He will destroy himself because he cannot handle the headaches or the confusion in his own being.

The most emblematic scene is in the mess hall of the prison

holding Cody. He sees a newcomer and asks for news of Ma. That question is relayed down a line of prisoners at the mess table, and then the stricken answer comes back, carried by prisoners horrified at their own message. When Cody learns that Ma is dead, he erupts—there is no other word, he is like a dancing puppet in neuronal frenzy. The emotion is human but the drive comes from insanity. The other actors and the extras were amazed at Cagney's wildness, and the scene ends on this force of nature with half a dozen guards trying to restrain him.

Yet this wonder was nearly spoiled. Jack Warner was reluctant to make it an expensive scene. Instead of a mess hall he wanted to set it in a chapel with just a few extras. Walsh asked for the studio machine shop as the setting and a few hundred extras, guaranteeing to get the scene in half a day.[8] Grudgingly, Jack agreed. It may be that that pressure stimulated everyone in one of the essential moments in Warners history. We have always wanted to idealize gangsters, and that reveals something reckless in us, something that was catered to in the movies. It is still hard not to be impressed by *White Heat*, to the point of demented exultation when Cody explodes with, "I made it Ma! Top of the world!" But I don't think it's a movie that ever inspired kids to love gangsters—watching *Lear* does not set you up to be a king. That Cagney and Margaret Wycherly were not even nominated only helps us appreciate how in the dark we can be at the movies.

There were mixed feelings over the film. Bosley Crowther ruminated at the bitter irony of a gangster story still being applauded.[9] Cagney himself had grown troubled by his outlaw reputation. This was the spirit of reform in which he had wanted to show Cody's pain and his damage. He wrote a personal promo for the picture: "*White Heat* points up dramatically and vividly the tremendous advances made in scientific detection. . . . It is bound to have a beneficial effect. . . . We are trying to make a gangster picture that will be a good gangster picture, a picture that will pay its way by helping deter crime."[10]

Perhaps it worked that way, or perhaps the film business—and Warners especially—was trying to avoid the truth, that it had defined and released a dangerous energy for all of us taught to dream, only to discover that the dream can hit a dead end. Decades later, we would have to learn how far Michael Corleone, Tony Soprano, and Walter White spoke to the unease and anger at being free yet imprisoned in a world of ruined dreams. We long to be outlaws, or to live by night.

There's a footnote to this part of the story. A few years after *White Heat*, a very good film was made, *Love Me or Leave Me*, based on the relationship between the singer Ruth Etting and her gangster lover, Marty "The Gimp" Snyder. It is a blend of musical and crime story such as Warner Bros were known for. And as written by Daniel Fuchs (who had done *The Hard Way* for Warners), it is a study of creativity and exploitation (of passion and slickness), trying to live together. The film has exceptional performances from Doris Day and Jimmy Cagney. It has songs like "Ten Cents a Dance" and "I'll Never Stop Loving You." Daniel Fuchs shared an Oscar for his script. But it was made for Metro-Goldwyn-Mayer by stars who had given up on Warners.

Studio identity was collapsing along with box office figures. By 1948, it was clear that the audience was in retreat, and that shift would accelerate as television became a new habit. In this crisis, the studio would try anything it could think of—3D, CinemaScope, films about teenagers, or even projects so artistic or perilous that a Warner brother would once have derided them. So it was that Warners made the movie of *A Streetcar Named Desire*.

The Tennessee Williams play had opened on Broadway in 1947 and been a sensation. This wasn't just because of the daring treatment of sexuality in ways bound to offend the Production Code, but because the production, by Elia Kazan, had identified a new level of naturalistic acting, associated with the Actors Studio, that would soon be called the Method. It was a play about Blanche DuBois, but the production had centered on Marlon Brando playing an emotional gangster—Stanley Kowalski sweeps the crockery off the dinner table the way Cagney had once served grapefruit for breakfast.

Streetcar's success encouraged wary talk of filming the play. That led to such fears of censorship that one mogul, Louis B. Mayer (father to the play's producer, Irene Selznick), had said everything would be all right if somehow the story could be given a happy ending. Lillian Hellman actually wrote such a script before Kazan reworked the Williams screenplay. With Charles Feldman as producer—a brilliant man, but seldom trusted—the picture was set up at Warners, with Kazan persuading himself that its integrity would be honored there. He made only one concession: Jessica Tandy, the stage Blanche, would be replaced by the starrier Vivien Leigh (who had played Blanche in London).

The film was shot and cut. There was a preview with some audience laughter at the wrong moments, so Kazan reedited to eliminate those spots. He was trying to stay on good terms with Jack Warner, though he feared Feldman was talking behind his back. But all parties were fearful of censorship. The Breen Office had recommended that Blanche "be searching for romance and security, and not for gross sex."[11] But a little bit of gross sex was edging into the mainstream, or seeming normal. Kazan told Jack, "I just saw [the film] again and I liked it. You will have your own impression, of course, but I thought it completely clean. Whatever there is of sex and violence is truthfully done, never exploited or sensationalized. And, I think it is full of the very Christian feeling of compassion and charity."[12]

Jack assented, but Kazan knew very well that in 1947–51,

the point of Tennessee Williams in America was not exactly to be clean or Christian; it was to turn over and freshen the hard, dry soil of our desire. The purpose was to shed poetry's light on behavior that had been subject to official repression, and widespread public ignorance—that was not so far from the revelation of Cody Jarrett in *White Heat*. So Kazan talked to Jack.

"I want your word," he said, "that this picture goes out as it is now. It's two hours and fourteen minutes, which is not long for a picture of this caliber. I want to go back to New York and see my family, and I don't want to be worried about what Charlie will do behind my back when I'm gone."

"The picture will go to the theatres as it is now," said Jack Warner.[13] There are some people never more alarming than when they make you a promise.

Streetcar was released on September 18, 1951, at two hours and two minutes. Cuts were made, as both Warner and Kazan had known they would be. You can say that Kazan felt betrayed, and he was as sensitive to that human trait as any natural betrayer. Kazan had expected it, and he had wanted to make the movie. It's a good picture and our fullest record of that historic production. Vivien Leigh is fragile in it, yet she holds her own with Brando's lunging energy. The prisoner is finally more interesting than the captor. *Streetcar* was nominated for twelve Oscars: it won for Leigh, for Karl Malden and Kim Hunter, and for the art direction. The film earned $8 million eventually on a cost of $1.8 million. What else do you want? The film of *Streetcar* was a compromise, but in the eyes of Jack Warner, that was a happy ending.

How else are movies made? The affronted artist needs someone to blame for his own compromise, and Jack was perfect casting in that part. What happened to Kazan's uneasy trust reminds me of a story told by the writer and screenwriter Niven Busch.

John Wayne went to Warners, and he *never* made failures, but there he was in red ink! It was kind of a put-down to him. He knew there was skullduggery, so he wouldn't speak to Jack Warner. He said, "Don't even mention his name!" For a couple of years if he saw Warner at a benefit, he'd walk out. He couldn't speak to him in a parking lot. Finally at some party Warner corners Wayne. He sticks out his hand and says, "Duke, you've been avoiding me." Wayne says, "That's right." "What happened, Duke? What went wrong?" Duke says, "Jack, it's very simple; you screwed me." Warner says, "Duke, I know, but that would have happened anyway. And we're your friends."[14]

What else did you expect? If Kazan had been betrayed by Jack Warner over twelve minutes on *Streetcar*, he still went back to him with the plea to make *East of Eden*.

As for Wayne, he was one of those actors who formed his own company, Batjac, releasing his pictures through Warners. That led to a group of intriguing films, including *The High and the Mighty, Hondo, Track of the Cat*, and eventually *The Searchers*, made by John Ford.

East of Eden may be the best film Kazan ever made, and many believe *The Searchers* was the peak of John Wayne's career. The one is an unguarded parable of fraternal rivalry, with one brother sent away so that another can rule, and the other is the story of a loner brother who goes to the ends of the earth to be avenged, who thinks of killing his defiled niece, and who harbors guilt because he loved—and maybe even had for a moment—his own brother's wife.

These are films made at Warner Brothers as the studio business was coming apart, and they provide oblique insight into what can drive a brother. They are both stories in which we become emotionally attached to tyrants of sentiment who behave with unbridled selfishness, and self-pity, in the name of wish fulfillment. At the end of *The Searchers*, the door closes on

Ethan Edwards, shutting him out of the homestead and committing him to the desert. It is a just verdict on a man not quite fit for company. But our hearts go with him, out there, into a lonely place where fantasy prevails. One might grow up a little unbalanced on films like these. You have to allow that Jack was a little crazy.

Jack Warner himself

17

Jacob's Ladder

IN 1955, Hirsch was seventy-three, Aaron was seventy, and Jacob was sixty-two. Schmuel had been dead twenty-eight years in October, and he was the brother the other three loved, for he had died to make them great, and famous, and rich. Schmuel had become Sam, Aaron was Albert, Hirsch was Harry, and Jacob was Jack. When kids in the family asked Jack what the original family surname had been, he said he could no longer remember. They had become Warner Bros. But if anyone needed to ask, they went to Jack. Not only was he younger; he was in charge, in California, running the studio, a grinning dinosaur from old Hollywood.

Harry had always been the oldest and the firmest. He said he was a simple, honest man who believed in the family, its heritage, and all the old stories. He had been like a father to them. He lived in New York, and he was the president of the company. He had been true to his wife, Lea, and he had had three children—Lewis, who died in his twenties, and two daughters, Doris and Betty. Doris had married two directors, one at a time, Mervyn LeRoy and Charles Vidor, and Betty had married a young assistant in the company, Milton Sperling. Harry was doing all he could to stay in charge of the business and the family, which meant that every day and night he grieved over the wayward energies and attitudes of his kid brother, Jack.

Albert was, by every account, the most ordinary and habitual of men, without much in the way of personality or ambition. It was his single desire to live in Florida with his wife, Bessie. This was his second wife Bessie, the first having died of influenza. He had had no children. Albert's pleasure in life was to live simply and to go to the track. These things were aided by living in Miami. But he was also the treasurer of the company. It was said of him, "He was not a man who would hold back from belching at the table."[1] If he had people for dinner, he would be first at the table; he might sit down and start to eat before the guests were seated. He liked to study the racing form and watch Westerns on television. And if he had to go to New York, he would sit in his office and read the numbers.

Jack lived in Los Angeles, and he was the head of production at Warner Bros. He had seen essential assistants, Darryl Zanuck and Hal Wallis, walk away because they couldn't stand him, and he had decided that they had not been essential. He ran more and more of the show himself, just as he had hired nearly everyone on the lot. In turn, those people endured or despised him. They called him bad names; they sometimes fought with him in the courts; they rarely trusted him; but they did agree that more or less Jack ran the show and had the hunches and the luck that made it work. It was said he could assess a script in just a few minutes without reading the whole thing. All you had to do with Jack was live with his smile, his restlessness, his boasts, his corny jokes, and his urge to sing to you—

and watch your back, because Jack might do anything to you, if only because you were his friend.

Just thank God you weren't his brother.

He had a grand house on Angelo Drive, where he lived with his wife, Ann.[2] She had made the house like a southern mansion, with a hint of Monticello, wrought-iron gates, a golf course, and a Versailles parquet floor. The house was Ann's production. It turned out that a lot of the antiques were fake, made to order at the Warners art department.

To remind you, Ann was Jack's second wife; he was her second husband. First of all, Jack had been married to Irma, and they had had a son, Jack Jr., born in 1916. But Jack had drifted from his duty; he had been unfaithful many times, and he had found Ann Boyar Page, who already had a daughter, Joy. Jack and Ann had begun their affair in about 1933, and they had a daughter, Barbara, in 1934 they were not actually married until 1936.

The affair, and the other affairs in Jack's career, as well as the divorce and the illegitimate child, had horrified Harry. Such things only confirmed the lack of character and reliability he had detected in Jack from an early age. As a result, Harry was not just disapproving of Ann, but inclined to ignore her. And since he was the declared head of the family, his attitude prevailed as something like an orthodoxy. The person most trapped in this situation was Jack Jr. He loved his mother and his father, and he tried to show respect for Ann. But his stepmother did not trust him, and she made it plain to Jack that he should be equally suspicious. So Jack Jr. was hired for a time at the studio, but then his own father told him to get out. He was rehired, and then fired again. Jack and Harry had a kind of mutual hatred that only brothers understand. For Jack to be disapproved of and disdained was the gravest injury. Harry was going to have to be punished.

Warner Bros had been a great factory system, and in the first years after the war it had flourished. But then the business deteriorated rapidly. This malaise went across the entire industry. Warners resisted better than any other studio.

They were still making a range of high-class entertainment: they let John Huston go to Mexico to shoot a yarn about chasing gold, *The Treasure of the Sierra Madre*, with Bogart, Walter Huston, and Tim Holt (both Hustons won Oscars); *Life with Father*, a popular family story with William Powell and Irene Dunne; *The Fountainhead*, for which the studio had allowed Ayn Rand to write her own screenplay, with Gary Cooper as the intransigent architect (he was Rand's choice when the studio had wanted Bogart); *The Flame and the Arrow*, for which they had made a deal with Burt Lancaster's production company to have Burt as a Robin Hood–like figure in old Lombardy; and *Captain Horatio Hornblower*, directed by Raoul Walsh, with Gregory Peck as a rather repressed English sea captain fighting Napoleon (Virginia Mayo played the female lead in both these adventures). There was also *Strangers on a Train*, a timely revival of Alfred Hitchcock's career after a few flops, in which Robert Walker gives one of the great performances in a Warners film.

The studio grasped the unruly phenomenon of James Dean, and had done his three pictures—*East of Eden; Rebel Without a Cause*, where Jack himself had believed enough in Dean to replace the early black-and-white footage with color; and *Giant*, more sprawling than the title promised, but earning $39 million on a cost of $6 million. Director George Stevens had wanted Alan Ladd in Dean's part, but Jack stood out for the difficult kid.

Warners had embraced Sid Luft's attempt to rescue the career of his wife, Judy Garland, in *A Star Is Born* (1954), when that venture relied on Judy being credible as an ingénue lead at thirty-two. The picture had wonders, but Jack had told his people to drop some of them, to make it shorter—and still it had been classified as a failure. They had made *The Bad Seed*

(1956), with Patty McCormack starring and Mervyn LeRoy directing, which is still one of the blackest movies ever made about an American child. Warners risked *Baby Doll*, from Tennessee Williams, with Carroll Baker sucking her thumb in a broken crib for a film condemned by the Catholic Legion of Decency. But more and more of us longed to be condemned.

It was still a brave studio. But by 1954, no one could miss the decline of the picture business or fail to see that Warner Bros remained a rich asset likely to lose value in the years ahead, even if the brothers had not been as old as they were, as out of touch, or as inclined to go to the races.

So what happened was businesslike, sensible, and predictable. But that wasn't enough. It had passion, too, malice and triumph. Jack began to suggest cashing out, taking the bounty that founding brothers deserved, and moving into what could be called retirement. Even Harry allowed that that might be a good idea. So Jack talked to an old ally, the Boston banker Serge Semenenko, about a scheme to buy out the partners. In the early summer of 1956, the brothers sold ninety percent of their stock to the Semenenko syndicate, with assurances to one another that they would all be out of there. Harry was suspicious. He was always wary of Jack, and he could tell that the kid's spirit was no less cunning than it had ever been. He was still having affairs with young women, and Ann, who had been his mistress once herself, could detect his old pattern of faithless behavior. I suspect Harry guessed what was coming.[3]

Jack had made a secret deal with Semenenko whereby, once the deal was done, he would reemerge, repurchase his own shares and more, and declare himself president of Warner Bros. Harry would be shafted, Jack would be in charge.

There was no fraud, no crime. It was more personal than that. The three brothers would share $22 million from the sale. This was a matter not of money but of power and control. There are different family versions of what happened, and of the degree of surprise. But most of them include heavy fore-boding on Harry's part. They also see the transaction as a movie story. The news broke that Jack had bought back in, and that he would be the new president. Seeing the newspaper headline, "Harry turned pale. He dropped the paper, grabbed the edge of the table, and fell to the floor."[4] He was taken to the hospital for observation—it was a heart attack, it was a stroke? It was a coup and a collapse. Rea Warner said that Jack might as well have put a gun to her Harry's head.[5]

Apparently, Harry came away with $8 million, but he suf-fered a series of strokes. On August 23, 1957, Harry and Rea celebrated their golden wedding anniversary. There was a party. Everyone was there, Jack Jr. included, but no one was certain Jack would show up. Jack Jr. gave an account of what followed.

> I was sitting in the living room with Harry when to my sur-prise the door swung open to admit my father. He bounced into the room exuding good cheer and jollity, his unnaturally black hair and thin mustache glistening. He stepped close to his brother and tried to say something of little consequence. Hoping Harry would perhaps notice him. Harry did notice . . . and he did the only thing he could still do. He closed his eyes tightly, shutting his brother from sight—and two big tears slowly rolled down his sunken cheeks. My father sud-denly stopped speaking, stood stiffly in front of his brother, who had communicated in the only way left to him. Then, with his face suddenly gone bright red, my father turned and almost ran out of the silent room. I reached over to hold my uncle's hand for a while until the tears stopped.[6]

Harry died on July 27, 1958, of a cerebral occlusion. He was seventy-six. There was a big funeral, but Jack was at his house in Antibes, and he sent a message saying he could not attend. Rea spoke out at the funeral. "Harry didn't die," she said. "Jack killed him."[7] There are close-up lines that people need to say, which others wait to hear. They are the heritage of movie melodrama, and why should the family that had created Bette Davis not be ready to utter such a line? How long had they waited to be heard?

A few nights later, still in the south of France, Jack left the Cannes casino in the early hours of the morning. He was in the habit of gambling more and more, and no one knows how he fared there. But he would play most nights, and he told anyone who asked that he had broken even. That night, at around 2 a.m., Jack crashed his car, an Alfa Romeo, into a truck. He was thrown forty feet out of his car and remained in a coma for several days.[8] Jack Jr. hurried to the south of France to be with him, but then it was said that the son caused grave offense by not seeing Ann Warner first and by telling the press that his father might die. Jack recovered, and that's when he fired Jack Jr. for the second time.

When he got back in Los Angeles, Jack Warner was in sole charge of a famed movie studio that—as he had warned his brothers—was going bust. Once there, he did not exercise the same close control. He had associates who did a lot of the managing for him. The most notable of these was Steve Trilling, who had been at the studio since the late 1920s.

By the 1950s, it was reckoned by insiders that no one handled Jack better than Trilling. He "ran the business of Warner Bros," observed the actor L. Q. Jones. "Jack Warner gave bad speeches and insulted people; Steve Trilling saw that A, B and C got done." Until one day, with Jack in France again, Trilling drove up to the studio gate and was told he could not enter. He had been fired. Everyone agreed he had given his life to the company. He committed suicide a couple of years later.[9]

Jack also appointed William T. Orr (who was married to Joy Page, his wife's daughter from her first marriage) to head a new television division. That was an area of entertainment that

Warners had been neglecting, but Orr was an industrious executive who launched series like *Route 66*, *Cheyenne*, and *Maverick*, which were important new sources of revenue and which made use of a Burbank studio that had fewer films to make.

In the early sixties, one film shone a toxic light on what was happening to the romance of movies. The director Robert Aldrich heard of a novel by Henry Farrell, *What Ever Happened to Baby Jane?*[10] It was about the Hudson sisters, movie stars once, who had grown up deadly rivals, living on some mysterious past grievance, cut off from reality in their decaying mansion. It was *Sunset Blvd* on the brink of being a horror film. Aldrich bought the rights, set a script in motion, and offered one of the parts to Joan Crawford (he had directed her a few years earlier in *Autumn Leaves*). Crawford saw the point immediately and guessed that Bette Davis was the obvious casting to play her sister.

The two actresses were not as old as the novel called for: in 1962, Davis was fifty-four and Crawford fifty-eight. But they had so much in common: their faded eminence—they were both great stars in decline; their involvement with Warners; and the unstoppable legend of their rivalry. However the film turned out, casting the two of them as warring sisters guaranteed media coverage.

Jack Warner had turned the venture down when Aldrich approached him. Was there some tact in the boss that shrank from this sibling cruelty? Or was he nervous about "two old broads" meaning enough at the box office? A new production company, Seven Arts, agreed to make the film, and the boss there, Eliot Hyman, imposed tough terms on the two stars. Crawford did it for $40,000 and ten percent of the producer's profits. Davis went for $60,000 and five percent of those profits. Aldrich agreed to make the picture for $850,000. After all, it was only the ladies, a house, a beach, and a dead parakeet. It didn't need to cost much. At which point, Jack Warner agreed to distribute the result. He gave a luncheon where he posed for pictures with the two actresses who had done so much for him. They called him a father figure who had given them grief in the past, but who was their friend again.

The picture opened in October 1962, just as the Cuban missile crisis was subsiding, and it was an event, earning $9 million. The public reveled in the humiliation of the stars and in the notion that these goddesses of a former age were crazy, vicious relics. The actresses prospered on the picture, but they were being admitted to a brand of gloating horror that made fun of them. At the same time, Warners did an honest tough film: *Days of Wine and Roses*, about liquor. Director Blake Edwards plus stars Jack Lemmon and Lee Remick were all in AA. And the film's ending stayed grim: Remick walks off into the night, a lost cause. Jack Warner called for a "happy ending," but Lemmon left town before it could be filmed.

Jack had his own swan song planned, and he meant it to be as lush as *Baby Jane* had been macabre. From the moment he saw the show on Broadway in 1956, he had loved *My Fair Lady*. It brought out the singer in him, and he thought it obvious that the show (2,717 performances) was bound to be a smash on screen. He would produce it himself, he promised William Paley, who owned the rights. Jack paid $5.5 million (almost the total cost of *Giant*) for that privilege, and reckoned on a film that would cost $15 million.[11]

It was not an easy project. Warner considered getting Vincente Minnelli to direct, but finally he gave the task to George Cukor. Alan Jay Lerner did the script, from his own musical and from the George Bernard Shaw play *Pygmalion*—there was little room for fresh thoughts. But Cukor quarreled with the appointed designer, Cecil Beaton, and the film is heavier-handed than anyone would wish. Jack had thought of Cary Grant for Henry Higgins and even Jimmy Cagney as Doolittle. But then he abided by the stage casting of Rex Harrison and Stanley Holloway.

He would assert himself, or be somebody, over the role of Eliza. Julie Andrews had played the part on stage in ways that defied thought of improvement. She had sung the songs and made them her own. She could have danced all night. But she had not yet done a movie. So Jack chose Audrey Hepburn instead: "There was nothing mysterious or complicated about that decision," he would say. "With all her charm and ability, Julie Andrews was just a Broadway name known primarily to those who saw the play. But in Clinton, Iowa, and Anchorage, Alaska, and thousands of other cities and towns in our fifty states and abroad you can say Audrey Hepburn, and people instantly know you're talking about a beautiful and talented star."[12]

He agreed to pay Hepburn $1 million when still uncertain whether her voice could carry the songs. Hepburn was under great stress: her marriage to Mel Ferrer was ending; she felt the burden of matching the stage success falling on her shoulders; and then Jack told her that her voice was not good enough. Marni Nixon would dub the songs.

The movie of *My Fair Lady* opened on November 8, 1964. Its $17 million budget turned into earnings of $70 million. It won Jack and Warners the third Best Picture Oscar of his regime. George Cukor got the Oscar as Best Director. But Audrey Hepburn was not even nominated. In the meantime, Disney had taken the chance of giving Julie Andrews a movie debut, in a picture called *Mary Poppins*. At the Oscar ceremonies where *My Fair Lady* won Best Picture, and Audrey presented the Best Actor Oscar to Rex Harrison, Julie Andrews received the actress Oscar. From the stage, with that lovely smile of hers, she said how much she owed to Jack Warner, "for making it all possible." He had to grin.

He had been building a grand finale for himself. To coincide with *My Fair Lady* and what he anticipated as its success, he compiled and published his memoir, *My First Hundred Years in Hollywood* (1965). It was not a reliable work: it omitted altogether the coup in which he had taken over from Harry; it told uncertain stories and delivered one-liners instead of being an attempt at history. Jack had not written all the book, but he had read it because he longed to believe it. It was a 332-page press release that ended on a vague embrace for family and strangers in the dark. *My Fair Lady*, he said, was, for the brothers,

> the end product of their dreams, the reward for their years of disappointment and hunger and work and want. It belongs to Ben Warner, weary on his cobbler's bench, hocking his watch and his horse because he knew his sons were right. It belongs to Pearl Warner, cooking and washing and scrubbing floors and enduring life in a peddler's wagon so her kids could hold their heads high. It belongs to Sam and Harry and Albert and Milton [a brother who had died in 1915] and Dave [another brother, who had died in 1939] in exchange for what they paid to make the promise of Warner Brothers come true. [The five sisters were omitted. Women are the final, outcast immigrants.]
>
> And it belongs to you who believed in us, for without you and all the rest I could not have told you about my first hundred years in Hollywood.[13]

The End? Exit music? Kol Nidre?

Not quite. There is a coda to the book, for Jack or the publisher had persuaded Ann to add a page: "In the more than thirty years I have been with Jack I have seen a man, supposedly shy and aloof, go out of his way to give courage and confidence to so many men and women as they played their part in building the name of Warner Brothers."[14]

Presumably, that grouping would have to include Jackie Park, the mistress Jack had taken to the London opening of *My Fair Lady*. He had introduced her that evening as having "a heart of gold and a snatch to match."[15] There are lines that stick in your head. A few years later he dropped Jackie and gave her a parting check for $5,000.

Jack L. Warner did sell the studio, in 1966, to Seven Arts, with $32 million coming to him personally. He rejoiced in that sum, but observers noted that he was soon lost with so little to do and no one to compete with. He attempted to preside over *Bonnie and Clyde*, which he understood was a gangster picture, even if one where the dame fired guns, too. The old man was unimpressed by the movie. He couldn't quite see it or hear it, let alone work out its purpose.

Its star and producer, Warren Beatty, took the film to Jack's house on Angelo Drive to show it to him, but Warner started going to the bathroom after the first reel. What is this stuff? the boss wondered. Beatty told him, "It's an homage to Warners gangster films." And Jack fired back, "What the hell is an homage?"[16]

Bonnie and Clyde was a rhapsody for beautiful kids in a stricken land who just wanted to be somebody—it was the immigrant dream, the one that parents, priests, rabbis, and teachers had advised against. But this time the kids robbed banks and shot anyone trying to stop them; they discovered love or sex and having their pictures taken; and if they were headed for a shoot-out where they were turned to chaff and fragments—wasn't that going to be the best death scene ever? The insolence was a philosophy in which the old hope for law and order was gone with the wind. It was the explosiveness that had always been hanging on Jolson's "Wait a minute!" or Leslie Crosbie's being ready to fire a hundred shots if her gun had had them.

To the racing soundtrack of "Foggy Mountain Breakdown," *Bonnie and Clyde* opened in 1967, and became a success after initial dismay gave way to enthusiasm, and after Beatty had persuaded Warners to sell the film with conviction, because he was a new somebody. In London, Beatty told the projectionist to play the gunfire extra loud. But Jack never understood how close to his old heart the film was. He was losing his touch. In the same year, his "personal production" of *Camelot* (directed by Joshua Logan) was a disappointment. Jack chose Richard Harris and Vanessa Redgrave, instead of Richard Burton and Julie Andrews, who had done it on stage.

Albert Warner died in Miami in November 1967 after a day at the track. He went home, sat down in front of the TV and had a stroke.

Jack died on September 9, 1978, after strokes had left him blind and helpless. He was eighty-six, and he didn't recognize people. Only the ghost of Harry might have revived him. Jack could be a jerk—he couldn't be much else—but nobody's perfect, and he had led and bamboozled the best studio there ever was. If there were bodies left in the streets, there always had been in Warner pictures.

Warner Brothers went on; you can say it's still there, in movies, television, music, and eternal branding. But the studio system is gone, and no one makes its movies now. Warner Bros had its share of trash, but few of its films were boring or pretentious. For a moment, they told our story as well as their contemporaries, those nifty automobiles, good for a getaway or taking a sweetheart to the beach. With luck, you were young at the right time—1927 to 1967, more or less—and you were as naïve and cocksure as Cagney, Bette, or Bugs, top of the world and horny.

America has become a tedious doom-ridden country now. But in those precious years it hated to be boring. It would kiss you if it hadn't just washed its hair.

---

1. An Introduction

1. On *Gentleman's Agreement*, see Steven Bach, *Dazzler: The Life of Moss Hart* (2001), 276; *Elia Kazan: A Life* (1988), 331–34; Mel Gussow, *Don't Say Yes Until I Finish Talking: A Biography of Darryl F. Zanuck* (1971), 158.

2. John Gregory Dunne, *The Studio* (1968), 242.

3. Ibid., 244.

4. Gussow, *Don't Say Yes*, xvii.

5. Orson Welles and Peter Bogdanovich, *This Is Orson Welles* (1992), ed. Jonathan Rosenbaum, 296.

6. Ibid., 274–75.

7. Director Edward Sutherland's Columbia Oral History quotes Chaplin saying, "I think I might have Jewish blood. I notice that my characteristics are very Semitic, my gestures are, my thinking is certainly along money lines." This is quoted in Kenneth S. Lynn, *Charlie Chaplin and His Times* (1997), 20.

8. In Alan LeMay's original novel, "Ethan" Edwards is named

Amos. Apparently the movie rejected one Jewish name for another because Amos was thought likely to remind viewers of *Amos 'n' Andy*. See Glenn Frankel, *The Searchers: The Making of an American Legend* (2013), 256.

2. The Greatest Moment?

1. Stephen Karnot, reader's report, December 11, 1941, quoted in Aljean Harmetz, *Round Up the Usual Suspects: The Making of Casablanca* (1992), 17. See also Noah Isenberg, *We'll Always Have Casablanca* (2017).

2. Hal Wallis, with Charles Higham, *Starmaker: The Autobiography of Hal Wallis* (1980).

3. Kati Marton, *Great Escape* (2007), in which Michael Curtiz is one of nine case studies of Hungarians who left Hitler's Europe.

4. Don Siegel, *A Siegel Film: An Autobiography* (1996).

5. Casey Robinson interview, *Backstory: Interviews with Screenwriters of Hollywood's Golden Age* (1986), ed. Pat McGilligan, 306–8.

6. Julius J. Epstein interview, *Backstory* (1986), 185.

7. Ibid., 189–90.

8. Harmetz, *Round Up the Usual Suspects*, 138–60.

9. Hal Wallis to Steve Trilling, February 5, 1942, *Inside Warner Bros, 1935–1951* (1985), ed. Rudy Behlmer, 199.

10. Sylvia Plath, "Daddy," *Ariel* (1965), 49–51.

3. What Are Brothers For?

1. Elia Kazan, *A Life* (1988), 534.

2. Kazan's ugliness is his own claim. In *A Life*, he says this (41): "I remember wondering what the hell was wrong with me anyway. My looks? My goddamn foreign looks? Those Anglos making the choices, what did they think? That I was a Jew boy? Yes, I looked like one. Was that it? Jews and blacks weren't taken into fraternities at Williams in 1926. Or was it something about my character? Was I clearly a freak of some kind? Was it something I couldn't see or understand that made me so absolutely unacceptable? My jittery sexuality—had they sensed that? Or was it something simpler, like my bowlegs, my acne, my big butt? What?"

All those questions pile up in the resentment felt by Cal in *East of Eden*.

3. Jack Warner, *My First Hundred Years in Hollywood* (1965), 15.

4. The family narrative is assembled from these books: Warner, *My First Hundred Years in Hollywood*; Cass Warner Sperling, *The Brothers Warner: The Intimate Story of a Hollywood Studio Family Dynasty* (1998); Richard Schickel and George Perry, *You Must Remember This: The Warner Bros Story* (2008); Bob Thomas, *Clown Prince of Hollywood: The Antic Life and Times of Jack L. Warner* (1990).

5. This aphorism has many sources or versions, from La Rochefoucauld to Gore Vidal, and from Somerset Maugham to Francis Coppola (whose sense of brothers animates the first two parts of *The Godfather*).

6. Leo Rosten, from his Columbia Oral History, quoted in Neal Gabler, *An Empire of Their Own: How the Jews Invented Hollywood* (1988), 121.

7. Joshua Logan, *Movie Stars, Real People, and Me* (1978), 1. Benny had evidence: *The Horn Blows at Midnight* (1945), for Warners, starring Benny, had been a famous flop.

8. Gabler, *An Empire of Their Own*, 147.

9. On Lina Basquette, Sperling, *The Brothers Warner*, 343; Lina Basquette, *Lina: DeMille's Godless Girl* (1990).

10. Sperling, *The Brothers Warner*, 207.

11. Mel Gussow, *Don't Say Yes Until I Finish Talking: A Biography of Darryl F. Zanuck* (1971), 36.

4. Family Dinner

1. The dinner is described in Cass Warner Sperling, *The Brothers Warner: The Intimate Story of a Hollywood Studio Family Dynasty* (1998), 29–31, and it is referred to by Jack Warner, *My First Hundred Years in Hollywood* (1965), 52–54.

2. Sperling, *The Brothers Warner*, 31.

3. William Wyer said, "To get the full impact of the revolver being fired, I thought everything should be very quiet first." See Axel Madsen, *William Wyler* (1973), 203.

4. David Weddle, *"If They Move . . . Kill 'Em!": The Life and Times of Sam Peckinpah* (1994), 362.

5. Mustache

1. Jack Warner, *My First Hundred Years in Hollywood* (1965), 53.
2. Ibid., 283–84.
3. Ibid., 87–88.
4. Ibid., 61.
5. Norman Mailer, *The Deer Park* (1955), chapter 20. Mailer spent time in Hollywood when his first novel, *The Naked and the Dead*, attracted movie interest. After several missed chances, including a Charles Laughton script, it ended up, directed by Raoul Walsh, as a Warner Bros picture in 1958.
6. Jack Warner to Hal Wallis, March 8, 1934; *Inside Warner Bros, 1935–1951* (1985), ed. Rudy Behlmer, 15.
7. Warner, *My First Hundred Years in Hollywood*, 129.
8. John McCabe, *Cagney: A Biography* (1997), 89. The story goes that Jack Warner and an associate were once talking about Cagney in front of him, unaware that the actor understood some Yiddish from several years in show business. So, ever after, Cagney relished calling Jack the *shvontz*. The story is irresistible, but it requires that we believe Jack really could speak Yiddish or Hebrew. In *My First Hundred Years*, he boasts that as a boy he "had no interest in studying the history of the Hebrews or their language" (17). Harry could speak Hebrew, but Jack pulled the beard of the rabbi meant to teach him, and never saw the man again.

6. For Liberty?

1. Neal Gabler, *An Empire of Their Own: How the Jews Invented Hollywood* (1988), 129–31.
2. Cass Warner Sperling, *The Brothers Warner: The Intimate Story of a Hollywood Studio Family Dynasty* (1998), 60–65.
3. Ibid.
4. Jack Warner, *My First Hundred Years in Hollywood* (1965), 90.

7. Rinty

1. Mel Gussow, *Don't Say Yes Until I Finish Talking: A Biography of Darryl F. Zanuck* (1971), 16.

2. Ibid., 17.

3. Ibid., 21. See Darryl Francis Zanuck, *Habit and Other Short Stories* (1923).

4. Susan Orlean, *Rin Tin Tin: The Life and the Legend* (2011), 62.

5. Ibid., 11.

8. Mama, Darlin'

1. Jack Warner, *My First Hundred Years in Hollywood* (1965), 181.

2. Ibid., 179.

3. Scott Eyman, *The Speed of Sound: Hollywood and the Talkie Revolution, 1926–1930* (1997), 129.

4. Quoted ibid.

5. Cass Warner Sperling, *The Brothers Warner: The Intimate Story of a Hollywood Studio Family Dynasty* (1998), 125.

6. Ernst Lubitsch to Harry Warner, January 29, 1926, *Inside Warner Bros, 1935–1951* (1985), ed. Rudy Behlmer, 336.

7. Harry Warner to Jack Warner, January 25, 1926, ibid., 37.

8. See Gene Fowler, *Good Night, Sweet Prince* (1944); Margot Peters, *The House of Barrymore* (1990).

9. *The Memoirs of Will H. Hays* (1955), 390.

10. Ibid. 391.

11. Warner, *My First Hundred Years in Hollywood*, 174–75.

12. See Alban Emley, *Mistah Jolson* (1951), 47.

13. Eyman, *The Speed of Sound*, 11–22.

14. Mel Gussow, *Don't Say Yes Until I Finish Talking: A Biography of Darryl F. Zanuck* (1971), 41.

9. Now

1. Casey Robinson interview, *Backstory: Interviews with Screenwriters of Hollywood's Golden Age* (1986), ed. Pat McGilligan, 297–98.

2. Darryl F. Zanuck, *The Hollywood Reporter*, December 1932, quoted in *Inside Warner Bros, 1935–51* (1985), ed. Rudy Behlmer, 9.

3. *I Am a Fugitive from a Chain Gang*, screenplay (1981), ed. John O'Connor, 35–36.

4. See John Bright interview, *Tender Comrades* (1997), ed. Patrick McGilligan and Paul Buhle, 133.

5. Jack Warner, *My First Hundred Years in Hollywood* (1965), 218.

6. On *Baby Face* and the Code, see Thomas Doherty, *Pre-Code Hollywood: Sex, Immorality, and Insurrection in American Cinema, 1930–1934* (1999); Mick LaSalle, *Complicated Women: Sex and Power in Pre-Code Hollywood* (2000).

10. My Forgotten Man

1. Those first words, "Wait a minute . . . You ain't heard nothin' yet" apparently caused a sensation at the première. There seems to have been no hint that this would happen, for sound—apparently—was simply there to carry a song. So let's stress: "Wait a minute" were the very first words, not the famous catchphrase, and "Wait a minute" is crucial, for it signals the pulse of sound movie—what next? what now?

2. Michael Freedland, *Al Jolson* (1972); Robert Oberfirst, *Al Jolson: You Ain't Heard Nothin' Yet* (1980). And don't forget how in *A Moveable Feast* (1964), Hemingway reports an occasion, in Paris, when Zelda Fitzgerald asked him, "Ernest, don't you think Al Jolson is greater than Jesus?" I believe Hemingway took this as a sign of Zelda's madness, but perhaps she was simply better attuned to the moment.

3. Mel Gussow, *Don't Say Yes Until I've Finished Talking: A Biography of Darryl F. Zanuck* (1971), 52.

4. On Busby Berkeley, see Jeffrey Spivak, *Buzz: The Life and Art of Busby Berkeley* (2010).

5. Joan Blondell interview, *People Will Talk* (1985), ed. John Kobal, 191–92.

6. Jack Warner to Hal Wallis, October 5, 1933, *Inside Warner Bros, 1935–1951* (1985), ed. Rudy Behlmer, 15.

7. Blondell, *People Will Talk*, 190.

11. Be Somebody

1. F. Scott Fitzgerald, *The Great Gatsby* (1926), chapter IV.

2. W. R. Burnett, *Little Caesar* (1929).

3. Quoted in Cass Warner Sperling, *The Brothers Warner: The Intimate Story of a Hollywood Studio Family Dynasty* (1998), 167.

4. Ibid., 188.

5. W. R. Burnett interview, *Backstory: Interviews with Screenwriters of Hollywood's Golden Age* (1986), ed. Pat McGilligan, 57.

6. On Edward G. Robinson, see Robinson and Leonard Spigelgass, *All My Yesterdays: An Autobiography* (1973).

7. Burnett, *Backstory*, 58.

8. Ben Hecht, *A Child of the Century* (1954), 421.

9. On James Cagney, see John McCabe, *Cagney: A Biography* (1997); Patrick McGilligan, *Cagney: The Actor as Auteur* (1975).

10. Joan Blondell interview, *People Will Talk* (1985), ed. John Kobal, 186.

11. On *The Public Enemy*, see William Wellman Jr., *Wild Bill Wellman: Hollywood Rebel* (2015), 265.

12. Kenneth Tynan, "James Cagney," *Profiles* (1989), 22–23; originally in *Sight and Sound*, May 1951.

13. See Wellman, *Wild Bill Wellman*, 269–70; Mel Gussow, *Don't Say Yes Until I Stop Talking: A Biography of Darryl F. Zanuck* (1971), 46.

14. John Bright interview, *Tender Comrades* (1997), ed. Patrick McGilligan and Paul Buhle, 135.

15. David Stenn, *Bombshell: The Life and Death of Jean Harlow* (1993), 56; Blondell, *People Will Talk*, 190.

16. Jack Warner, *My First Hundred Years in Hollywood* (1965), 204.

17. Sperling, *The Brothers Warner*, 185.

12. Bette v. Everyone

1. Joan Blondell interview, *People Will Talk* (1985), ed. John Kobal, 187.

2. Bette Davis, *The Lonely Life* (1962), 11.

3. Graham Greene, *The Spectator*, June 19, 1936, in *Mornings in the Dark: The Graham Greene Film Reader* (1993), ed. David Parkinson, 111–12.

4. Davis, *The Lonely Life*, 142.

5. Ibid., 157.

6. Ibid., 159–69.

7. Ibid., 168.

8. Ibid., 174.

9. Ibid., 174–78.

10. Ibid., 182.

11. Ibid., 204; Axel Madsen, *William Wyler* (1973), 204–5.

12. Vincent Sherman interview, *People Will Talk*, 562.

13. Contracts and Company

1. Bette Davis to Jack Warner, December 5, 1940, *Inside Warner Bros, 1935–1951* (1985), ed. Rudy Behlmer, 239.

2. Rowland Leigh to Hal Wallis, March 28, 1936, ibid., 30.

3. Olivia de Havilland to Jack Warner, July 18, 1939, ibid., 98–99.

4. Jack Warner, August 12, 1943, ibid., 234.

5. On Clint Eastwood, see Patrick McGilligan, *Clint: The Life and the Legend* (1999).

6. George Raft to Jack Warner, June 6, 1941, *Inside Warner Bros*, 151.

7. Darryl F. Zanuck to Edward G. Robinson, October 26, 1932, ibid., 6–7.

8. Hal Wallis to Michael Curtiz, April 22, 1942, ibid., 202.

9. Andrew Sarris, *The American Cinema: Directors and Directions, 1929–1968* (1968), 174–76. His consideration of Curtiz includes this, talking about the director's decline from the early fifties onwards: "What the collapse of studio discipline meant to Curtiz and Hollywood was the bottom dropping out of routine filmmaking." There's truth in that, but does the range from *20,000 Years in Sing Sing* to *Mildred Pierce*, from *Yankee Doodle Dandy* to *Casablanca*, and from *Captain Blood* to *Life with Father* simply qualify as "routine"?

10. Joan Blondell interview, *People Will Talk* (1985), ed. John Kobal, 190.

14. Unafraid?

1. Jack Warner, *My First Hundred Years in Hollywood* (1965), 225–26. Jack also liked this Mizner story. The writer was dying, in an oxygen tent. "Well, this looks like the main event," he said. A priest approached him with the last rites, whereupon Mizner cracked, "Why should I talk to you? I've just been talking to your boss."

2. On *Heroes for Sale*, see William Wellman Jr., *Wild Bill Wellman: Hollywood Rebel* (2015), 277–79.

3. A. M. Sperber and Eric Lax, *Bogart* (1997), 80.

4. See Jerome Lawrence, *Actor: The Life and Times of Paul Muni* (1974).

5. Frank Nugent, *New York Times*, August 12, 1937.

6. Warner, *My First Hundred Years in Hollywood*, 248–49.

7. Ben Urwand, *The Collaboration: Hollywood's Pact with Hitler* (2013), 269.

8. Warner, *My First Hundred Years in Hollywood*, 235. However, a few years later, Jack was warning that any further sign of liquor on a Flynn set and he might "abrogate the entire contract and sue him for damages"; *Inside Warner Bros, 1935–1951* (1985), ed. Rudy Behlmer, 274 (June 1947).

9. See David Welky, *The Moguls and the Dictators: Hollywood and the Coming of World War II* (2008).

10. John Wexley interview, *Tender Comrades* (1997), ed. Patrick McGilligan and Paul Buhle, 711–12.

11. Frank Nugent, *New York Times*, April 29, 1939.

12. Manny Farber, "Mishmash," *Farber on Film: The Complete Film Writings of Manny Farber* (2009), ed. Robert Polito, 70.

13. Robert Stripling, Committee on House Un-American Activities Committee hearings, *Inside Warner Bros*, 289.

14. Jack Warner, ibid., 290.

15. On Ida Lupino and *The Hard Way*, see William Donati, *Ida Lupino: A Biography* (1996); Vincent Sherman interview, *People Will Talk* (1985), ed. John Kobal, 558.

16. On *Objective, Burma!* see Marilyn Ann Moss, *Raoul Walsh: The True Adventures of Hollywood's Legendary Director* (2011), 246–55.

17. Robert Lord to Jack Warner, August 29, 1945, *Inside Warner Bros*, 262–64.

18. Jack Warner to Robert Lord, August 31, 1945, ibid., 264.

19. I recommend Chuck Jones, *Chuck Amuck: The Life and Times of an Animated Cartoonist* (1989). But do wabbits wead?

15. Bogart

1. On Bogart, scc Λ. M. Sperber and Eric Lax, *Bogart* (1997).

2. Louise Brooks, *Lulu in Hollywood* (1982), originally in *Sight and Sound*, winter 1966–67. Brooks deflates the image of Bogie the loner: "Being myself a born loner, who was temporarily deflected from the hermit's path by a career in the theatre and films, I can state categorically that in Bogart's time there was no other occupation in the world that so closely resembled enslavement as the career of a film star."

3. W. R. Burnett, *High Sierra* (1940), chapter 1.

4. John Huston to Hal Wallis, March 21, 1940, *Inside Warner Bros, 1935–1951* (1985), ed. Rudy Behlmer, 126.

5. On *They Drive by Night*, see Sperber and Lax, *Bogart*, 126; William Donati, *Ida Lupino: A Biography* (1996), 60–64.

6. On Lauren Bacall, see Bacall, *By Myself* (1979).

7. Ibid., 79.

8. Slim Keith with Annette Tapert, *Slim: Memories of a Rich and Imperfect Life* (1990), 95–96.

9. Ibid., 78–83.

16. After the War, Before the End

1. On Joan Crawford, see Bob Thomas, *Joan Crawford: A Biography* (1978).

2. F. Scott Fitzgerald to Gerald Murphy, March 11, 1938, *The Letters of F. Scott Fitzgerald* (1963), ed. Andrew Turnbull, 447.

3. Tom Chapman to Roy Obringer, March 4, 1949, *Inside Warner Bros, 1935–1951* (1985), ed. Rudy Behlmer, 255.

4. Thomas, *Joan Crawford*, 146.

5. On Doris Day, see A. E. Hotchner, *Doris Day: Her Own Story* (1975).

6. Jerry Wald to Steve Trilling, June 15, 1946, *Inside Warner Bros*, 272.

7. Introduction, *White Heat* screenplay (1984), ed. Patrick McGilligan, 15.

8. Ibid., 28.

9. Bosley Crowther, *New York Times*, September 10, 1949.

10. John McCabe, *Cagney: A Biography*, 250.

11. Breen Office to Warner Brothers, April 28, 1950, *Inside Warner Bros*, 323–24.

12. Elia Kazan to Jack Warner, October 19, 1950, ibid., 326.

13. Elia Kazan, *A Life* (1988), 417.

14. Niven Busch interview, *Backstory: Interviews with Screenwriters of Hollywood's Golden Age* (1986), ed. Pat McGilligan, 106.

17. Jacob's Ladder

1. Cass Warner Sperling, *The Brothers Warner: The Intimate Story of a Hollywood Studio Family Dynasty* (1998), 171.

2. Jean Stein, *West of Eden: An American Place* (2016), 45–46.

3. On the deal, see *The Brothers Warner*, chapter 20.

4. Ibid., 307.

5. Ibid., 313.

6. Ibid., 312.

7. Ibid., 313.

8. Jack Warner, *My First Hundred Years in Hollywood* (1965), 3–5.

9. On Steve Trilling, see Marilyn Ann Moss, *Raoul Walsh: The True Adventures of Hollywood's Legendary Director* (2011), 364.

10. On *What Ever Happened to Baby Jane?* see Shaun Considine, *Bette and Joan: The Divine Feud* (1989), 307–44.

11. On *My Fair Lady*, see Patrick McGilligan, *George Cukor: A Double Life* (1991); Gavin Lambert, *On Cukor* (1972).

12. Warner, *My First Hundred Years in Hollywood*, 330.

13. Ibid., 331.

14. Ibid., 332.

15. Stein, *West of Eden*, 104–7.

16. On *Bonnie and Clyde*, see Mark Harris, *Scenes from a Revolution: The Birth of the New Hollywood* (2008), 326–27.

ACKNOWLEDGMENTS

Many people at Yale University Press helped with this book. That list is headed by John Donatich, Steve Zipperstein, and Ileene Smith. Erica Hansen presided over the project and knew where the letters of transit were (most of the time). Dan Heaton was tireless, enthusiastic, brilliant, and still an Arsenal supporter at every stage of the journey. Fred Kameny wrote a cogent and complete index, and proofreader Jack Borrebach swept up whatever spilled popcorn the editors and the author stepped over.

Away from the Press, I owe essential thanks to Michael Barker, Molly Haskell, Richard and Mary Corliss, to Niven Busch, to David Packard, Bruce Goldstein, and every movie theatre manager (going back to the Regal in Streatham in the 1940s) who knew I needed to see Warner Bros pictures. So start with *The Flame and the Arrow*, with a Bugs Bunny short.

Writers on film are expected to thank the directors, the writers, and the actors—on the assumption that they are artists. I do that, naturally, but I want to say that I learned just as much from the people who knew the process was a business for confident rascals, so go easy on any talk about art. Most of the best stories I've ever heard and repeated were told me by those business guys who crossed their fingers night and day that the matter of art might be forgotten. If Harry, Jack, Albert, and Sam had ever guessed the awkward truth about "art," they might have stayed home or settled for making shoes.

INDEX

Page numbers in *italics* refer to illustrations.